FRANCE
by Marcel Martin

GW00673471

£1.25/$3.50

In the same

Screen Series

edited by Peter Cowie
produced by The Tantivy Press

Eastern Europe
by Nina Hibbin

Sweden 1 and 2
by Peter Cowie

Germany
by Felix Bucher

The Gangster Film
by John Baxter

Japan
by Arne Svensson

A Concise History of the Cinema
(2 volumes) *edited by Peter Cowie*

The American Musical
by Tom Vallance

FRANCE

by Marcel Martin

A. Zwemmer Ltd, London
A. S. Barnes & Co, New York

Acknowledgements

The author and publishers wish to acknowledge their thanks to the following companies, individuals, and organisations who originally issued the photographs used in this volume: Anouchka Films, Georges de Beauregard, Bibliothèque de l'IDHEC, Giancarlo Botti, Brandon Films, Gilles Caron-Gamma, La Cinémathèque Française, Cocinor, Columbia Pictures, Continental-Films, Georges Dambier, Films La Boétie, Films du Carrosse, Films 13, Gala Film Distributors, Les Grands Films Classiques, Etienne Hubert, Limot, Lira Films, Roger Manvell, M-G-M, Mondial Films, Musée des Arts Décoratifs, Office du Livre de Cinéma, Parc Film/Madeleine Films (notably the colour photograph of *Les Demoiselles de Rochefort* by Hélène Jeanbrau), Paris Film Production, Rome Paris Films, M. Jean-Claude Romer, Sebricon Productions, Editions Seghers (Pierre Lherminier), Pierre Toussaint, Unifrance Film, Uninci, United Artists, and especially the Fédération Française des Cinés-Clubs. Most of the photographs come from the author's personal collection.

The author also wishes to thank Peter Cowie for his very helpful co-operation on the project.

Cover Stills
FRONT: Catherine Deneuve and Françoise Dorléac in LES DEMOISELLES DE ROCHEFORT
BACK: Jean Seberg and Jean-Paul Belmondo in A BOUT DE SOUFFLE

FIRST PUBLISHED 1971
Copyright © 1971
by Marcel Martin
SBN 302 02133 7 (U.K.)
SBN 498 07518 4 (U.S.A.)
Library of Congress
Cat. no: 69–14900
Filmset by Keyspools Ltd, Golborne, Lancs.
Printed by C Tinling & Co Ltd, Prescot & London

Introduction

The selection of the four hundred entries included in this dictionary is of course arbitrary and open to question. But the choice has stemmed from a desire to concentrate on both past and present, thus including the names of famous or underrated personalities in French cinema history as well as contemporary figures, among them those who may have only just begun their career but whose work indicates trends for the future.

The manuscript was closed for press on March 1, 1971, and films produced after that date are generally excluded.

Works Consulted

Index de la Cinématographie Française. Paris: 1947–1965.

La Saison cinématographique. Paris: 1955–1970.

Annuaire biographique du Cinéma. Paris: Contact Editions, 1963.

Sadoul, Georges. *Dictionnaire des cinéastes*. Paris: Editions du Seuil, 1965.

Dictionnaire du cinéma. Paris: Editions Seghers, 1962.

Jeanne, René, and Ford, Charles. *Dictionnaire du cinéma universel*. Paris: Editions Robert Laffont, 1970.

Colpi, Henri. *Le Cinéma et ses hommes*. Montpellier: Les Editions Causse, Graille et Castelnau, 1947.

Dictionnaires du nouveau cinéma français in *Cahiers du Cinéma* (Nos. 138, 155, 187), Paris.

Graham, Peter. *A Dictionary of the Cinema*. London: A. Zwemmer, 1968; New York: A. S. Barnes, 1968.

Anouk Aimée, Gérard Philipe and Gérard Séty in MONTPARNASSE 19

Main Entries

1 ACHARD, Marcel (1900 –   ). B:
Sainte-Foy-les-Lyon. Scriptwriter. The most
brilliant "Boulevard" playwright of the past
forty years. His dialogue is renowned for its
essentially Parisian flavour. Member of the
Académie française.

Main films: *Jean de la lune* (from his play),
*Mayerling, Orage, Alibi, Gribouille, L'étrange
M. Victor, Untel père et fils, L'Arlésienne,
Madame de . . ., Le Pays d'où je viens, La Femme
et le pantin, Les Amours célèbres* (one episode).

2 AGOSTINI, Philippe (1910 –   ). B:
Paris. Distinguished director of photography,
noted for the richness of his imagery. 1934:
entered cinema.

Main films (as dir. of phot.): *Un Carnet de
bal, Le Mariage de Chiffon* (co. Jean Isnard),
*Les Anges du péché, Lettres d'amour, Douce,
Premier de cordée, Les Dames du Bois de
Boulogne, Sylvie et le fantôme, Les Portes de la
nuit, Les dernières vacances, Pattes blanches,
Le Plaisir, Châteaux en Espagne, Du Rififi chez
les hommes, Si Paris nous était conté.* As
director: *Le Naïf aux quarante enfants, Tu es
Pierre, Le Dialogue des Carmélites, Rencontres,
Soupe aux poulets.*

3 AIMÉE, Anouk (1932 –   ). B: Paris.
RN: Françoise Sorya. Actress, admired for the
grace and romantic aura of her presence. She
had already been appearing in films for over a
decade when Demy's *Lola* revived her career
and made her one of the most intriguing French
stars of the Sixties.

Main films: *Les Amants de Vérone, Le
Rideau cramoisi, Les mauvaises rencontres,
Montparnasse 19, La Tête contre les murs, Les
Dragueurs, La dolce vita* (Fellini, Italy, 60),
Lola, Il Giudizio universale (De Sica, Italy, 61),

Il terrorista (De Bosio, Italy, 63), *Les grands
chemins, Un Homme et une femme, Un Soir un
train* (Delvaux, Belgium, 68), *The Appoint-
ment* (Lumet, U.S.A., 68), *Model Shop, Justine*
(Cukor, U.S.A., 69).

4 ALBICOCCO, Jean-Gabriel (1936 –
). B: Cannes. Director. Several shorts.
Fastidious film-maker, somewhat inclined to
aestheticism for its own sake.

Films: *La Fille aux yeux d'or, Le Rat
d'Amérique, Le grand Meaulnes, Le Cœur fou,
Le petit matin.*

5 ALEKAN, Henri (1909 –   ). B: Paris.
Director of photography. At first assistant to
Périnal, Schuftan, and Kelber (qq.v.). Admired
for the severe realism of his compositions. Also
dir. shorts, including *L'Enfer de Rodin* (58).

Main films: *La Bataille du rail, La Belle et la
Bête, Les Maudits, Une si jolie petite plage,*

Les Amants de Vérone, La Marie du port, Juliette ou la clef des songes, La meilleure part, Les Héros sont fatigués, Austerlitz, La Princesse de Clèves, L'autre Cristobal, Topkapi (Dassin, 64), *The Poppy Is Also a Flower* (T. Young, 66), *Mayerling* (T. Young, 68), *The Christmas Tree* (T. Young, 69), *Figures in a Landscape* (Losey, G. B., 70).

6 ALEXEIEFF, Alexandre (1901 –). B: Kazan. Painter, of Russian parentage; also stage designer and book illustrator; then animator, using his own patent method, "l'écran d' épingles," a board on which about one million pins are manipulated to achieve ghostly silhouette effects.

Films: *Une Nuit sur le Mont Chauve* (short, 32), *La belle au bois dormant* (puppets, 35), *En passant* (short, 43), *Le Nez* (short, 63). Also several commercials and advertising films, as well as the credit sequence for Welles's *The Trial*. Now working on a new short: *Tableaux d'une exposition* (from Moussorgsky).

7 ALLÉGRET, Marc (1900 –). B:

Basle. Journeyman director, with some pleasing films to his credit during the Thirties.

Main films: *Voyage au Congo* (medium length, with André Gide, 26), *Fanny, Lac aux dames, Orage, Gribouille, Entrée des artistes, L'Arlésienne, Futures Vedettes, L'Amant de Lady Chatterley, En effeuillant la marguerite, Les Parisiennes, Le Bal du Comte d'Orgel.*

8 ALLÉGRET, Yves (1907 –). B: Asnières. Brother of above. Director, noted for his harsh *naturalism* (q.v.).

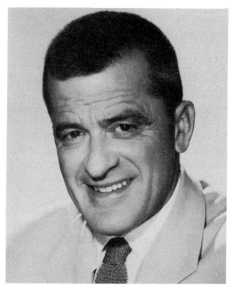

Main films: *Dédée d'Anvers, Une si jolie petite plage, Manèges, Les Miracles n'ont lieu qu'une fois, La jeune folle, Les Orgueilleux, La meilleure part, Germinal.*

9 ALLIO, René (1924 –). B: Marseille. Director. Also an excellent stage designer and director. An extremely original and sympathetic film-maker. Shorts include *La Meule* (62).

Films (also scripted): *La vieille dame indigne, L'une et l'autre, Pierre et Paul, Les Camisards.*

8

10 ANIMATION. Term applied to all forms of expression that refer to shooting *image by image* rather than the customary continuous shooting of regular cinema: cartoons (on celluloid); puppet films; drawing or scratching directly on the film (also painting, e.g. MacLaren); Alexeieff's pin board; films composed of still photographs.

Animation pre-dates the orthodox cinema. As early as 1890, Emile Reynaud had perfected his *théâtre optique*. From 1907 onwards, Emile Cohl was the pioneer of animation in its definitive form. In 1932, came the unique film of the Czech, Berthold Bartosch, *L'Idée* (in Paris), and the first film by Alexeieff (q.v.) on his pin board (*Une Nuit sur le Mont Chauve*).

1941: Paul Grimault (q.v.), the greatest French animator, begins his important career. During the Fifties, there was the prolific but artistically mediocre work of Jean Image, and some early cartoons, witty and meticulous, by Henri Gruel (q.v.). In the Sixties, the "Parisian school" composed of the Poles Walerian Borowczyk (q.v.) and Jan Lenica, the Englishman Peter Foldes, and the Italians Bettiol-Lonati-Bettiol. There was also something of a "new wave" led by Jean-François Laguionie, André Martin and Michel Boschet, Manuel Otero, Julien Pappé, Albert Pierru (scratching directly on the film), Piotr Kamler, and Robert Lapoujade.

11 ANNABELLA (1910 –   ). B: La Varenne. RN: Suzanne Charpentier. Graceful and attractive actress who starred in some memorable films of the Thirties. 1938 – 1950: U.S.A.

Main films: *Napoléon, Maldone, Le Million, Quatorze Juillet, Variétés, La Bandera, Hôtel du Nord.*

12 ANNENKOV, Georges (1901 –   ). B: Petropavlovsk. Costume designer, Russian by birth, celebrated for the discreet elegance of his work, especially in the films of Max Ophuls.

Annenkov has also worked for the theatre.

Main films: *Mayerling, La Duchesse de Langeais, Pontcarral, L'éternel retour, Patrie, La Symphonie pastorale, La Chartreuse de Parme, La Ronde, Madame de . . ., Lola Montès, Montparnasse 19.* Author of two books, looking back over his career: "En habillant les vedettes" (51), and "Max Ophuls" (62).

13 ANOUILH, Jean (1910 –   ). B: Bordeaux. Dramatist, scriptwriter, adapter, and dialogue supervisor.

Main films: *Monsieur Vincent, Pattes blanches, Caroline chérie, La Ronde.* As director: *Le Voyageur sans bagage, Deux sous de violettes.*

14 ANTOINE, André (1858 – 1943). B: Limoges. D: Paris. Stage director, pioneer of *naturalism* (q.v.) in the theatre circa 1885. Also directed some films, to which he applied his theories; he contributed to the spread of *realism* during the Twenties.

Main films: *Les Frères corses, Les Travailleurs de la mer, Le Coupable, La Terre, L'Arlésienne.*

ANTOINE, André-Paul (1892 –   ), his son. Scriptwriter. Also journalist and dramatist. Main films: *Les Mystères de Paris, La tendre ennemie, De Mayerling à Sarajevo, Le Carrefour des enfants perdus, French Cancan.*

15 ARCADY (1912 –   ). B: Sofia. Director of photography. A leading specialist in special effects and trick shots, particularly in short films on artistic subjects.

Main films: *Les Désastres de la guerre* (52), *Avec André Gide* (53), *Ledoux l'architecte maudit* (55), *Lettre de Sibérie* (58) etc. Also dir. of short documentaries, cartoons, and fiction films. Main films: *Léonard de Vinci* (52), *Images préhistoriques* (55), *Prélude pour voix, orchestre et caméra* (60), *L'Ondomane* (61), *Les Automanes* (65).

16 ARLETTY (1898–). B: Courbevoie. RN: Léonide Bathiat. Actress. At first a star of stage and music hall. In the cinema (from 1930) she became famous for her dash, her wit, and her irrepressible vulgarity, at their sharpest in the films of Marcel Carné*.

Main films: *Pension Mimosas, Faisons un rêve, Les Perles de la couronne, Hôtel du Nord*, Le Jour se lève*, Fric-frac, Madame Sans-Gêne, Les Visiteurs du soir*, Les Enfants du paradis*, Le grand jeu, Huis clos, L'Air de Paris, La Gamberge, The Longest Day* (Zanuck, U.S.A., 61).

17 ARNOUL, Françoise (1931–). B: Constantine (Algeria). RN: F. Gautsch. Actress, brought to prominence by *French Cancan*, but who has never been able to establish herself in the front rank of French stars.

Main films: *La Rage au corps, Napoléon* (54), *French Cancan, Si Paris nous était conté,*

Le Pays d'où je viens, Sait-on jamais?, Le Testament d'Orphée, La Morte-saison des amours, Vacances portugaises, Le petit théâtre de Jean Renoir.

18 ARTAUD, Antonin (1896–1948). B: Marseille. D: Ivry-sur-Seine. Writer, actor, stage director. A significant figure in the *avant-garde* (q.v.) movement, who also played a key role as a theorist with his book "Le Théâtre et son double," in which he set out his ideas of the "theatre of cruelty" and his visionary notions of film art. An unforgettable actor in *Napoléon* (27) and *La Passion de Jeanne d'Arc* (Dreyer, 28). Scripted *La Coquille et le clergyman*.

19 ARTHUYS, Philippe (1928–). Director. Also musician and talented composer. Wrote scores for *India* (Rossellini, 57), *Paris nous appartient, Madame se meurt* (sound effects), *Les Carabiniers, Le Vent des Aurès* (Lakhdar Hamina, Algeria, 67), *L'Opium et le* *bâton* (Ahmed Rachedi, Algeria, 69). Script-writer, composer, and director of some original and subtle features: *La Cage de verre, Des Christs par milliers.*

20 ASTRUC, Alexandre (1923 –   ). B: Paris. Director. At first journalist, novelist, and film critic. His theoretical writings have been of considerable importance. His concept of the *caméra-stylo* (q.v.), for instance, defined the purpose and style of the *nouvelle vague* that was to come. His shorts include: *Le Puits et le pendule* (for TV, 63), and *Evariste Galois* (65).

Films (also co-scripted*): *Le Rideau cramoisi*, Les mauvaises rencontres*, Une Vie*, La Proie pour l'ombre*, Education sentimentale, La longue marche*, Flammes sur l'Adriatique*.*

Antonin Artaud in NAPOLÉON (below). Alexandre Astruc (above)

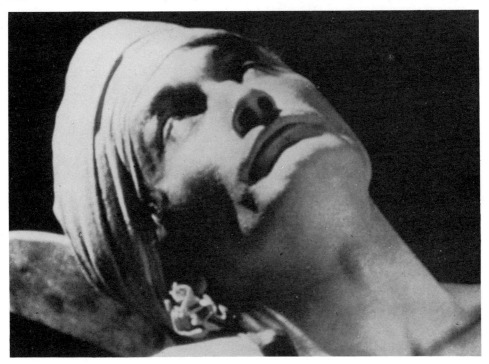

21 AUCLAIR, Michel (1922–). B: Koblenz. RN: Vladimir Vujović. Stage and screen actor, with a somewhat withdrawn, if solid personality.

Main films: *La Belle et la Bête, Les Maudits, Manon, Justice est faite, Le Fête à Henriette, Si Versailles m'était conté, Le Rendez-vous de minuit, Education sentimentale, Vacances portugaises.*

22 AUDIARD, Michel (1920–). B: Paris. Journalist, novelist, then scriptwriter. His dialogue is often brilliantly amusing, but always rather facile.

Main films: *Sang et lumière, Courte-tête, Mort en fraude, Les Misérables, Rue des Prairies, Le Baron de l'Ecluse, Un Taxi pour Tobrouk, Les Vieux de la vieille, Un Singe en hiver, Mélodie en sous-sol, Les Tontons flingueurs, La Métamorphose des cloportes.* Films as director: *Faut pas prendre les enfants du bon dieu pour des canards sauvages, Une Veuve en or, Elle boit pas, elle fume pas, elle drague pas mais elle cause, Le cri du cormoran le soir au-dessus des jonques.*

23 AUDRAN, Stéphane (1933–). B: Versailles. Stage and screen actress. Studied under Charles Dullin, Tania Balachova, and Michel Vitold. After a modest beginning, she has developed into an excellent performer, especially in the films of her husband, Claude Chabrol (q.v.)*, where her sophistication and confident beauty conceal deep emotional strain.

Main films: *Les Cousins*, Le Signe du lion, Les bonnes femmes*, Les Godelureaux*, L'œil du malin*, Landru*, Paris vu par . . .* (Chabrol episode)*, *La Ligne de démarcation*, Le Scandale*, Les Biches*, La Femme infidèle*, Le Boucher*, La Peau de torpedo, La Rupture*, Juste avant la nuit*.*

24 AUDRY, Jacqueline (1908–). B: Orange. Woman director. At first script-girl and then assistant. A conscientious film-maker; but her work lacks genuine personality.

Main films: *Les Malheurs de Sophie, Gigi, L'ingénue libertine, Olivia, Huis-clos, Mitsou, La Garçonne, Soledad, Le Lis de mer.*

25 AUMONT, Jean-Pierre (1913–). B: Paris. RN: J-P. Salomons. Actor, popular for his charm. The great "jeune premier" of the Thirties. Also starred in several Hollywood productions.

Main films (in France): *Jean de la lune, Lac aux dames, Maria Chapdelaine, Drôle de drame, Hôtel du Nord, Si Versailles m'était conté, Napoléon* (54), *Vacances portugaises.*

26 AUREL, Jean (1925–). B: Rasvolitza (Romania). Scriptwriter and dialogue writer.

Main films (as scr.): *Une Parisienne, Porte des Lilas, Le Trou, La Bride sur le cou.* As director: *14–18* and *La Bataille de France* (documentary reconstructions), then *De l'amour, Lamiel, Manon 70, Les Femmes, Etes-vous fiancée à un marin grec ou à un pilote de ligne?.*

27 AURENCHE, Jean (1904–). B: Pierrelatte. Noted scriptwriter, usually working in partnership with Pierre BOST (q.v.). At first wrote treatments for advertising shorts. Long collaboration with Autant-Lara (q.v.)*.

Main films (alone): *Madame Sans-Gêne, L'Affaire du Courrier de Lyon, Lettres d'amour*, Le Mariage de Chiffon*, Sylvie et le fantôme*, Vive Henri IV vive l'amour*, Journal d'une femme en blanc*, Le Rouge et le blanc*.* With Pierre Bost: *Douce*, La Symphonie pastorale, Le Diable au corps*, Au-delà des grilles, Occupe-toi d'Amélie*, L'Auberge rouge*, Jeux interdits, Le Blé en herbe*, Le Rouge et le noir*, Gervaise, La Traversée de Paris*, La Femme et le pantin, En cas de malheur*, Le Joueur*, La Jument verte*, Les Régates de San Francisco*, Le Bois des amants*,*

Opposite: Stéphane Audran

Tu ne tueras point*, Le Meurtrier*, Le Magot de Joséfa*, Les Amitiés particulières, Paris brûle-t-il?, Le Franciscain de Bourges*.

28 AURIC, Georges (1899 –). B: Lodève. Well-known composer, and member of the "Groupe des Six" with Honegger (q.v.), Milhaud, Poulenc. A familiar figure in the *avant-garde* (q.v.) of the Twenties, he appeared briefly as an actor in Clair's *Entracte*, together with Satie, Picabia, Marcel Duchamp, and Man Ray.

Main films: *Le Sang d'un poète, A nous la liberté, Lac aux dames, Gribouille, Entrée des artistes; Macao, l'enfer de jeu; L'éternel retour, La Belle et la bête, La Symphonie pastorale, Les Jeux sont faits, Les Parents terribles, Orphée, Le Salaire de la peur, Du Rififi chez les hommes, Gervaise, Celui qui doit mourir, Les Aventures de Till l'Espiègle, Lola Montès, Le Mystère Picasso, Les Espions, Les Sorcières de Salem, Les Bijoutiers du clair de lune, La Princesse de Clèves, Thomas l'Imposteur, La grande vadrouille.* Auric also wrote the music for several English films (*Dead of Night, Caesar and Cleopatra, Queen of Spades, Passport to Pimlico, The Lavender Hill Mob, The Innocents* etc.) as well as Hollywood productions (*Moulin Rouge, Roman Holiday, Bonjour Tristesse, Aimez-vous Brahms?* etc.).

29 AURIOL, Jean-George (1907 – 1950). B. and D: Paris. A talented critic whose premature death in a car accident was a considerable loss to the French cinema. Founded the *Revue du Cinéma*, first series (1928 – 1931) and second series (1946 – 1949). Scripted: *Lac aux dames, Le Carrefour des enfants perdus* etc.

30 AUTANT-LARA, Claude (1903 –). B: Luzarches. A typical director of "cinéma de qualité," respected for his social and political satires. At first set and costume designer on *Don Juan et Faust, L'inhumaine, Nana* etc.

Films: *Fait-divers* (short, 23), *Construire un feu* (short, 25), *Ciboulette, My Partner Mr. Davis* (in G.B.), *Fric-frac* (co. M. Lehmann), *Mariage de Chiffon, Lettres d'amour, Douce, Sylvie et le fantôme, Le Diable au corps, Occupe-toi d'Amélie, L'Auberge rouge, Les sept péchés capitaux* (one episode), *Le Blé en herbe, Le bon dieu sans confession, Le Rouge et*

Madeleine Robinson and Marguerite Moreno in Claude Autant-Lara's DOUCE

le noir, Marguerite de la nuit, La Traversée de Paris, En cas de malheur, Le Joueur, La Jument verte, Les Régates de San Francisco, Le Bois des amants, Tu ne tueras point; Vive Henri IV, vive l'amour; Le Comte de Monte-Cristo, Le Meurtrier, Le Magot de Joséfa, Journal d'une femme en blanc, Le nouveau journal d'une femme en blanc, Le plus vieux métier du monde (one episode), *Le Franciscain de Bourges, Les Patates, Le Rouge et le blanc.*

31 AVANT-GARDE. Aesthetic concept that implies experimentation and a rejection of the traditional categories of commercial cinema. In the French cinema, the *avant-garde* is traditionally linked with the years 1925 –

1930, when the influence of Dada and Surrealism were at their height. Two main tendencies can be discerned: firstly, the abstract (influenced by the Germans Ruttmann and Fischinger), figurative films based on ideas of rhythmical or musical character, among them *Le Ballet mécanique* (Fernand Léger), *Arabesque* (Germaine Dulac), *La Marche des machines* (Eugène Deslaw), *Cinq minutes de cinéma pur* (Henri Chomette).

The second tendency was a *surrealist* one, centring on the manipulation of visual or psychoanalytical symbols and on a distortion of reality: *La Coquille et le clergyman* (Germaine Dulac), *L'Etoile de mer* (Man Ray), *Entracte* (René Clair), *Un Chien Andalou* and

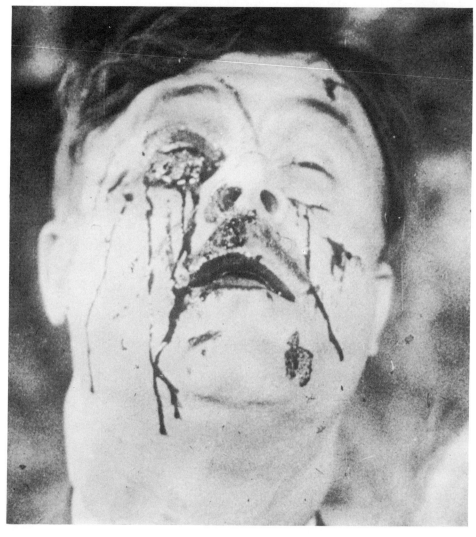

Gaston Modot in Buñuel's L'AGE D'OR

L'Age d'or (Luis Buñuel), and *Le Sang d'un poète* (Jean Cocteau).

A third tendency is covered by the term *impressionism* (q.v.) with its parallels to the French school of painting.

32 AZNAVOUR, Charles (1924 –   ). B: Paris. RN: Charles Aznavourian. Actor, at first composer and singer. His screen roles have shown him to be a gifted actor.

Main films: *La Tête contre les murs, Les*

Dragueurs, Le Passage du Rhin, Tirez sur le pianiste, Un Taxi pour Tobrouk, Le Rat d'Amérique, La Métamorphose des cloportes, Le Temps des loups, The Adventurers (Gilbert, U.S.A., 70), *The Games* (Winner, Britain, 70), *Un beau monstre.*

Charles Aznavour in LE TESTAMENT D'ORPHÉE

33 BAC, André (1905 –   ). B: Paris. Well-known director of photography since 1945, with a sober, rigorous style.

Main films: *Le 6 Juin à l'aube, Noces de sable, Le Point du jour, Occupe-toi d'Amélie, L'Auberge rouge, Le bon dieu sans confession, Le Dialogue des Carmélites, La Guerre des boutons, Bébert et l'omnibus, Les Copains.*

34 BACHELET, Jean (1894 –   ). B: Azans. Director of photography, brought up in Russia, whose reputation has been built on a precise and lively style that probably derives from his experience as a newsreel cameraman (from 1912).

Main films: *La Fille de l'eau, Nana, La petite marchande d'allumettes, La petite Lise, Tire au flanc, Crainquebille, Madame Bovary, Le Crime de M. Lange, La Règle du jeu, Nous les gosses, La Poison, La Vie d'un honnête homme.*

35 BADAL, Jean (1927 –   ). B: Budapest. Director of photography who spent his youth in Hungary (cameraman on Feher's *A Sunday Romance*, 57, under his real name of János Badal). A major talent whose work is always realistic and uncluttered.

Main films: *Les mauvais coups, Le Rendez-vous de minuit, Education sentimentale, Ballade pour un voyou, Les Cœurs verts, Playtime, L'Une et l'autre, La Fiancée du pirate, Le Grabuge, Le dernier saut, La Promesse de l'aube* (Dassin, 70), *L'Humeur Vagabonde.* Also *Adventure Starts Here* (Donner, Sweden, 65).

36 BALIN, Mireille (1911 – 1968). B: Monte Carlo. Actress, famous during the Thirties for her parts as a temptress and *femme fatale.*

Main films: *Pépé le Moko, Gueule d'amour, Naples au baiser de feu, Macao l'enfer du jeu, L'Assedio dell'Alcazar* (Genina, Italy, 40), *Dernier atout.*

37 BARATIER, Jacques (1918 –   ). B: Montpellier. Director. At first shorts, including *Métier de danseur* (53), *Paris la nuit* (co. Jean Valère, 55). His features are influenced by the curious, burlesque poetry of the literary *avant-garde.*

Films: *Goha le simple, La Poupée, Dragées au poivre* (also co-scripted), *L'Or du duc* (also scripted), *Le Désordre a vingt ans* (also scripted), *Piège, La Décharge.*

38 BARDOT, Brigitte (1934 –). B: Paris. Actress. At first model. Probably the most famous French film star of all time, a "sex kitten" during the Fifties and a mature *comédienne* in the Sixties. Has also worked in the theatre. 1952: film *début*.

Main films: *Futures vedettes, Les grandes manœuvres, En effeuillant la marguerite, Mio figlio Nerone* (Steno, Italy, 56), *Et Dieu créa la femme, Une Parisienne, Les Bijoutiers du clair de lune, En cas de malheur, La Femme et le pantin, Le Testament d'Orphée, Babette s'en va-t-en guerre, La Vérité, La Bride sur le cou, Vie privée, Le Repos du guerrier, Le Mépris, Viva Maria, Masculin-féminin, A cœur joie, Une ravissante idiote, Les Histoires extra-ordinaires* (Malle episode), *Shalako* (Dmytryk, U.S.A., 68), *Les Femmes, L'Ours et la poupée, Les Novices, Boulevard du rhum.*

39 BARRAULT, Jean-Louis (1910 –). B: Le Vésinet, Seine. Stage and screen actor, as well as a highly competent theatre director (since 1935). Head of the Renaud-Barrault Company. 1932: stage *début*. His ardent, youthful enthusiasm enlivened several classics of the Thirties and Forties.

Main films: *Mayerling, Jenny, Un grand amour de Beethoven, Drôle de drame, La Symphonie fantastique, Les Enfants du paradis, La Ronde* (50), *Si Versailles m'était conté, Le Dialogue des Carmélites, Le Testament du Dr. Cordelier, The Longest Day* (Zanuck, U.S.A., 61), *La grande frousse, Chappaqua* (Rooks, U.S.A., 66).

40 BARSACQ, Léon (1906 – 1969). B: Crimea. D: Paris. Set designer (brother of André, stage designer and producer); admired for the elegance, precision, and historical authenticity of his sets.

Main films: *Le Marseillaise, Les Enfants du*

Opposite: Brigitte Bardot

paradis, Boule de suif, L'Idiot, Le Silence est d'or, La Beauté du diable, Belles de nuit, Les Diaboliques, Les grandes man uvres, Porte des Lilas, Tout l'or du monde, Symphonie pour un massacre, Raspoutine, Diaboliquement vôtre.

41 BAUDRIER, Yves (1906 –). B: Paris. Composer whose music is delicate and subtle. Baudrier has been responsible for several film and TV scores.

Main shorts: *La grande pastorale* (Clément, 36), *Le Tempestaire* (Epstein, 47), *Stéphane Mallarmé* (Lods, 60). Features: *La Bataille du rail, Les Maudits, Le Château de verre, La Nuit est mon royaume, Les sept péchés capitaux* (two episodes), *Le Monde du silence.*

42 BAUR, Harry (1880 – 1943). B. and D: Paris. Stage and screen actor. One of the most dignified and imposing figures of the prewar period.

Main films: *David Golder, Poil de carotte, Les Misérables, Crime et châtiment, Un grand amour de Beethoven, Un Carnet de bal, Volpone, L'Assassinat du Père Noël.*

43 BAZIN, André (1918 – 1958). B: Angers. D: Nogent-sur-Marne. The most important and most revered film critic since the war. Co-founder (1951) and co-Editor-in-chief (1951 – 58) of *Cahiers du Cinéma*. His premature death dealt a great blow to French criticism, which was stimulated by his rigorous and intelligent essays. His principal theoretical writings were published under the title of "What Is Cinema?" (four volumes, 1958–62, partially translated into English by Hugh Gray). Also books on Orson Welles, Vittorio De Sica, and Jean Renoir (the latter unfinished at his death).

44 BEAUREGARD, Georges de (1920 –). B: Marseille. Producer. At first journalist. A dynamic personality who gave many

Nouvelle Vague directors their chance to make features.

Main films: *Death of a Cyclist* (Bardem, Spain, 1955), *A bout de souffle, Lola, Cléo de 5 à 7, Une Femme est une femme, Le petit soldat, Adieu Philippine, Le Doulos, Les Carabiniers, Landru, Le Mépris, Le Vampire de Düsseldorf, La 317ème section, Pierrot le fou, La Religieuse, La Ligne de démarcation, Objectif 500 millions.*

45 BEAUSOLEIL, Claude (1928 –). B: Asnières. Director of photography. A masterly craftsman when shooting in colour.

Main films: *Marie-Soleil, Le Bonheur, L'Enfance nue, Léa l'hiver.*

46 BECKER, Jacques (1906 – 1960). B. and D: Paris. Director. A major figure whose early death was a substantial loss to French cinema. At first assistant to Jean Renoir (q.v.) from

Above: Jacques Becker. Below: Becker's LE TROU

whom he learnt humanity and the poetry of the everyday.

Shorts include: *Le Commissaire est bon enfant* (co. Pierre Prévert, 35), *Le Gendarme est sans pitié* (35). Features (all co-scripted except*): *Dernier atout, Goupi mains rouges, Falbalas, Antoine et Antoinette, Rendez-vous de Juillet, Edouard et Caroline, Casque d'or, Rue de l'Estrapade*, Touchez pas au grisbi, Ali Baba et les 40 voleurs, Les Aventures d'Arsène Lupin, Montparnasse 19*, Le Trou*. Becker also began work on *L'Or du Cristobal* (39), but this was later completed by, and credited to, Jean Stelli.

47 BECKER, Jean (1933 –). B: Paris. Director. Son of above. At first assistant to his father and to Henri Verneuil (q.v.).

Films (also scripted*): *Un nommé La Rocca*, *Echappement libre*, Pas de caviar pour tante Olga*, Tendre voyou*.

48 BELL, Marie (1900 –). B: Bègles. A great stage tragedienne, whose ample presence and domineering manner have made her a force to be reckoned with in her few cinema appearances.

Main films: *L'Homme à l'Hispano, Le grand jeu, Un Carnet de bal, La Charrette fantôme, Le Colonel Chabert, La bonne soupe, Vaghe stelle dell'orsa* (Visconti, Italy, 65).

49 BELLON, Loleh (1926 –). B: Paris. Stage actress, pupil of Tania Balachova, with a refined, mysterious air to her playing.

Main films: *Le Point du jour, Le Parfum de la dame en noir, Maître après dieu, Casque d'Or, Le bel âge.*

50 BELLON, Yannick (1924 –). B: Biarritz. Sister of above. Film editor and director. Made her name with a fine short, *Goémons* (48), and a longish documentary on the writer, *Colette* (50). Other shorts:

Varsovie quand même (54), *Pastorale interrompue* (54), *Les Hommes oubliés* (57). Her style is sharp and observant.

51 BELMONDO, Jean-Paul (1933 –). B: Neuilly. Actor, first on stage and then in films. The number one star of the *Nouvelle Vague* thanks to his "tough" image and his puckish sense of humour.

Main films: *Les Tricheurs, A bout de souffle, A double tour, Classe tous risques, Moderato cantabile* (Brook, France, 60), *Léon Morin, prêtre; Une Femme est une femme, Un nommé La Rocca, Un Singe en hiver, Cartouche, Le Doulos, L'Aîné des Ferchaux, Dragées au poivre, Peau de banane, L'Homme de Rio, Les tribulations d'un Chinois en Chine, Week-end à Zuydcoote, Pierrot le fou, Paris brûle-t-il?, Tendre voyou, Le Voleur, Ho!, Le Cerveau, La Sirène du Mississipi, Un Homme qui me plaît, Borsalino, Les Mariés de l'An Deux, Le Casse.*

52 BENAYOUN, Robert (1926 –). Critic and film historian, an expert on animation and zany comedy (with several books to his credit). Has directed two interesting features: *Paris n'existe pas, Sérieux comme le plaisir.*

53 BENAZERAF, José (1922 –). B: Casablanca. Producer, then director of films distinguished by the originality and audacity of their subject matter.

Main films: *Le Cri de la chair, La Drogue du vice, L'Enfer sur la plage, Joe Caligula, Un épais manteau de sang, Le désirable et le sublime.*

54 BENOIT-LÉVY, Jean (1888 – 1959). B. and D: Paris. Director. Specialist in documentaries and educational films. Was attached to UNESCO as an adviser on film matters (1946 – 49). Published two books: "Le Cinéma d'enseignement et l'éducation" and "Les grandes missions du cinéma."

Some four hundred shorts, then main features: *La Maternelle* (co. Marie Epstein), *La Mort du cygne.*

55 BÉRARD, Christian (1902 – 1949). B. and D: Paris. Painter, art director, costume designer. Worked a great deal with Jouvet (q.v.) and above all with Cocteau (q.v.). He worked mainly for the theatre but also on some Cocteau films*.

Main films: *La Belle et la bête*, *L'Aigle à deux têtes*, *Les Parents terribles*, Amore* (episode *La Voix humaine*, Rossellini, 48).

56 BERGER, Nicole (1937 – 1967). Extremely talented actress who was prematurely killed in a car crash. Her appeal stemmed from her grave but delicate personality.

Main films: *Celui qui doit mourir, En cas de malheur, Les Dragueurs, Tirez sur le pianiste, La Dénonciation, La Permission* (Van Peebles, France, 67).

57 BERNARD, Paul (1898 – 1958). B: Villeneuve-sur-Lot. Stage and screen actor, usually associated with suave and cynical characters.

Main films: *Pension mimosas, Lumière d'été, Les Dames du Bois de Boulogne, Les Maudits, Pattes blanches.*

58 BERNARD-AUBERT,   Claude (1930 –). B: Durtal. Director. At first a war correspondent in Indochina, an experience that inspired his first film. Made several socially committed films and then returned to commercial productions.

Films: *Patrouille de choc, Les Tripes au soleil, Les Lâches vivent d'espoir, A fleur de peau, Poliorkia ou les moutons de Praxos, Le Facteur s'en va-t-en guerre, L'Ardoise.*

59 BERRI, Claude (1934 –). B: Paris. RN: Claude Langmann. Director. At first concentrated on shorts, among them *Le Poulet* (62) and a sketch for the portmanteau production *La Chance et l'amour.* His features cast a humorous glance at the Jewish background in which he grew up.

Films (also scripted): *Le vieil homme et l'enfant, Mazel Tov ou le Mariage, Le Pistonné, Le Cinéma de Papa* (also acted). Prod. *L'Enfance nue.*

60 BERRY, Jules (1883 – 1951). B: Poitiers. D: Paris. RN: Jules Paufichet. Stage actor, pupil of André Antoine. He was brilliant at playing cynical, satanic characters whose wit and sly charm exerted an extraordinary fascination. Berry was a member of that great acting generation (Baur, Guitry, Jouvet, Raimu, Marguerite Moreno etc.) who dominated French films of the Thirties and Forties.

Main films: *Le Crime de M. Lange, Le Voleur de femmes, Le Mort en fuite, Le Jour se lève, La Symphonie fantastique, Les Visiteurs du soir, Marie-Martine, Le Voyageur de la Toussaint, Portrait d'un assassin, Histoires extraordinaires* (49).

Michel Simon and Alain Cohen in Claude Berri's LE VIEIL HOMME ET L'ENFANT

61 BERTHOMIEU, André (1903 – 1960). B: Rouen. D: Paris. Prolific director, responsible for some sixty films, few of which were of lasting value. A competent technician rather than a true *auteur*, he published his ideas on film in a book entitled "Petit essai de grammaire cinématographique" (46). At first singer and later assistant to René Hervil.

Main films: *Ces Dames aux chapeaux verts, Le Crime de Sylvestre Bonnard, Les Ailes brisées, La Mort en fuite, Les nouveaux riches, La chaste Suzanne, La Neige sur les pas, L'Ange de la nuit, J'ai 17 ans, Le Bal des pompiers, La Femme nue, Préméditation.*

62 BIANCHETTI, Suzanne (1894 – 1936). B. and D: Paris. An actress of considerable talent who died young and who is commemorated with an annual prize carrying her name and awarded to the best young actress in French cinema.

Main films: *Jocelyn, Les Mystères de Paris, Madame Sans-Gêne, Napoléon, Verdun vision d'histoire, Le père Goriot, L'appel du silence.*

63 BLAIN, Gérard (1930 –). B: Paris. Stage and screen actor, usually associated with violent and complex-ridden characters. Has worked a lot in Italy.

Main films: *Avant le déluge, Les Mistons, Le beau Serge, Les Cousins, La Peau et les os, I Delfini* (Maselli, Italy, 60), *Il Gobbo* (Lizzani, Italy, 60), *Hatari!* (Hawks, U.S.A., 62), *Les Vierges, Joe Caligula, Un Homme de trop.* As director (also scripted): *Les Amis.*

64 BLANCHAR, Pierre (1896 – 1964). B: Philippeville. D: Paris. Stage and screen actor. His hard, headstrong features, combined with an often exaggerated manner, have best suited him for violent or visionary roles.

Main films: *Jocelyn, Le Joueur d'échecs, L'Atlantide* (Pabst, 32), *Crime et châtiment* (34), *Un Carnet de bal, Pontcarral, Patrie, La Symphonie pastorale, Docteur Laënnec.*

65 BLANCHE, Francis (1921 –). B: Paris. Chubby French star of minor film farces and character actor in bigger projects. One of the busiest figures in French cinema. Also active in cabaret and music hall. His loud, uncouth Nazi officer in *Babette s'en va-t-en guerre* established him as a comedy star.

Main films: *La Jument verte, Un Couple, Certains l'aiment froide, La Française et l'amour, En plein cirage, Snobs, Les Parisiennes, Les Vierges, Un Drôle de paroissien, Dragées au poivre, Les Tontons flingueurs, La Tulipe noire, La Chasse à l'homme, Les plus belles escroqueries du monde, Les Gorilles, Les Barbouzes, Le Chance et l'amour, La bonne occase, Pas de caviar pour tante Olga, Les Compagnons de la marguerite, Le plus vieux métier du monde, Belle de jour, La grande lessive, Erotissimo, L'Etalon, Etes-vous fiancée à un marin grec ou à un pilote de ligne?* As director and actor: *Tartarin de Tarascon.*

66 BLIER, Bernard (1916 –). B: Buenos Aires. Stage and screen actor. Supporting

roles in the Thirties. Now a solid, Gabin-like performer in gangster films and comedies.

Main films: *Entrée des artistes, Hôtel du Nord, Le Jour se lève, La Symphonie fantastique, Dédée d'Anvers, Quai des Orfèvres, Avant le déluge, Les Misérables, Le Joueur, Marie-Octobre, Le Monocle noir, Germinal, Les Tontons flingueurs, Cent mille dollars au soleil, Peau d'espion, Un Idiot à Paris, L'Etranger* (Visconti, Italy/France/Algeria, 67), *Faut pas prendre les enfants du bon dieu pour des canards sauvages, Le Distrait, Biribi.*

67 BLIER, Bertrand (1939 –). B: Paris. Director. Son of above. At first assistant. The younger Blier has so far failed to establish himself as a major director.

Film: *Hitler, connais pas, Si j'étais un espion.* Also only scripted *Laisse aller, c'est une valse.*

68 BLIN, Roger (1907 –). B: Neuilly-sur-Seine. Stage and screen actor. Much admired as an *avant-garde* theatre producer. As an actor he specialises in portraying disturbed or visionary characters.

Main films: *Entrée des artistes, La Symphonie fantastique, Les Visiteurs du soir, Douce, Orphée, Notre-Dame de Paris, Les Tripes au soleil.*

69 BOISROND, Michel (1921 –). B: Châteauneuf-en-Taymerais. Director. At first assistant. Prolific but mediocre film-maker.

Main films: *Cette sacrée gamine, Une Parisienne, Faibles femmes, La Française et l'amour* (one episode), *Les Amours célèbres, Les Parisiennes, Comment réussir en amour, La Leçon particulière, Du Soleil plein des yeux, On est toujours trop bon avec les femmes.*

70 BOISSET, Yves (1939 –). Director, at first critic and assistant. His early work shows a brilliant and confident approach to cinema.

Films: *Coplan sauve sa peau, Cran d'arrêt, Un Condé, Le Cobra.*

71 BONNARDOT, Jean-Claude (1923 –). B: Paris. Director, at first only of shorts. Made his name with an important political film, *Morambong*. Also: *Ballade pour un voyou.*

72 BOROWCZYK, Walerian (1923 –). B: Kwilcz (Poland). Director and animator. 1946 – 1951: studied painting at Academy of Fine Arts, Cracow. Since 1959: lived in France. An outstanding animator, with a grotesque sense of humour and superb technique. Also designer of film credits (*Les Félins, La Vie de Château*).

Shorts: (in collab. with Jan Lenica) *Once upon a Time* (57), *Love Requited* (57), *Dom* (58), (alone) *The School* (58), *Les Astronautes* (co. Chris Marker, 59), *Le dernier voyage de Gulliver* (60), *Le Concert de M. et Mme Kabal* (62), *Holy Smoke* (63), *Renaissance* (63), *L'Encyclopédie de Grand'maman* (63), *Les Jeux des anges* (64), *Le Dictionnaire de Joachim* (65), *Rosalie* (66), *Gavotte* (68), *Diptyque* (68), *Le Phonographe* (69). Features: *Le Théâtre de M. et Mme Kabal* (cartoon), *Goto, l'île d'amour* (live action), *Blanche* (live action).

73 BOST, Pierre (1901 –). B: Lasalle. Novelist, dramatist, and a leading scriptwriter, usually working in collab. with Jean AURENCHE (q.v.).

Main films (alone): *Patrie, Les Jeux sont faits, Le Château de verre.* With Jean Aurenche: see entry 27.

74 BOULANGER, Daniel (1922 –). Prominent *Nouvelle Vague* scriptwriter, admired for his black humour.

Main films (dialogue only*): *Les Jeux de l'amour, Le Farceur, Cartouche, L'Amant de cinq jours, Peau de banane, Echappement libre, L'Homme de Rio*, Les Tribulations d'un Chinois en Chine, Marie-Chantal contre le Dr Kah, Le Roi de cœur* (also acted), *La Route de Corinthe*, Histoires extraordinaires* (*William Wilson* episode)*, Le Diable par la queue, Les Caprices de Marie.* Also actor (usually a heavy) in *A bout de souffle, Tirez sur le pianiste, La Mariée était en nour, Domicile conjugal La Maison sous les arbres.*

Michel Bouquet and Maurice Ronet in LE DERNIER SAUT

75 BOUQUET, Michel (1926–). B: Paris. Stage and screen actor, with a strong and unusual personality, especially in Chabrol's work*.

Main films: *Monsieur Vincent, Pattes blanches, Manon, Les Amitiés particulières, Lamiel, La Route de Corinthe*, La Mariée était en noir, La Femme infidèle*, La Sirène du Mississipi, Le dernier saut, Borsalino, La Rupture*, Un Condé, Comptes à rebours, Juste avant la nuit*, L'Humeur vagabonde.*

76 BOURGUIGNON, Serge (1928–). B: Maignelay. Director. At first assistant, then concentrated on shorts (*Le Sourire*, 60, etc.). A somewhat mannered film-maker with lyrical pretensions.

Films (also scripted): *Les Dimanches de Ville-d'Avray, The Reward* (in U.S.A.), *A cœur joie*.

77 BOURVIL, André (1917–1970). B: Petrot-Vicquemare. D: Paris. RN: André Raimbourg. Famous comedian. At first baker, farm worker, music hall personality, and singer. A jovial star of French farce, at his most popular during the Sixties.

Main films: *Miquette et sa mère, Seul dans*

Paris, *Les trois mousquetaires, La Traversée de Paris, Les Misérables, Le Miroir à deux faces, La Jument verte, Fortunat, Tout l'or du monde, Un drôle de paroissien, Le Corniaud, La grande vadrouille, Le Cerveau, The Christmas Tree* (Young, France/Italy, 69), *L'Etalon, Le Cercle rouge, Le Mur de l'Atlantique.*

78 BRASSEUR, Claude (1936–). B: Paris. Stage and screen actor (son of Pierre), with a lively and amusing personality. 1956: film *début.*

Main films: *Le Pays d'où je viens, La Bride sur le cou, Le Caporal épinglé, Dragées au poivre, Bande à part, Lucky Jo, Germinal, Un Homme de trop, Le Portrait de Marianne, Trop petit mon ami.*

79 BRASSEUR, Pierre (1905–). B: Paris. Stage and screen actor, famous for the wit, irony, and bravura strength of his performances.

Main films: *Madame Sans-Gêne, La Fille de l'eau, Les deux timides, Quai des brumes, Lumière d'été, Adieu Léonard, Les Enfants du paradis, Le Pays sans étoiles, Les Portes de la*

nuit, *Les Amants de Vérone, Maître après dieu, Les Mains sales, Porte des Lilas, La Tête contre les murs, La Loi* (Dassin, Italy, 58), *Les Yeux sans visage, Il bell' Antonio* (Bolognini, Italy, 60), *Dialogue des Carmélites, Les grandes familles, Pleins feux sur l'assassin, Les bonnes causes, La petite vertu, Les Oiseaux vont mourir au Pérou; Goto, l'île d'amour.*

80 BRAUNBERGER, Pierre (1905–). B: Paris. Prominent producer whose career spans virtually the entire modern French cinema, from the Twenties to date. Associated with shorts as well as features. Own company: Les Films de la Pléiade. Own cinema: Le Panthéon (Paris).

Main films: *Nana* (also acted), *Rien que les heures, Voyage au Congo, Tire au flanc, La Fille de l'eau, Un Chien Andalou, L'Age d'or, On purge bébé, La Chienne, Une Partie de campagne, Les Maîtres fous, Moi un noir, L'Eau à la bouche, Tirez sur le pianiste, Vivre sa vie, Muriel, L'Amérique insolite, La Pyramide humaine, La Dénonciation, Un Cœur gros comme ça, Un Homme et une femme, Mamaïa, Erotissimo, Fantasia chez les ploucs.*

Above: Florence Carrez in Bresson's
PROCÈS DE JEANNE D'ARC. At left:
Robert Bresson

81 BRESSON, Robert (1907–). B:
Bromont-Lamothe. A director of major stature,
admired for the purity and rigour of his style as
well as for the psychological and moral gravity
of his work. Read philosophy and classics at
university. Then painter.

Films: *Les Affaires publiques* (medium
length), *Les Anges du péché, Les Dames
du Bois de Boulogne, Journal d'un curé de
campagne, Un Condamné à mort s'est échappé,
Pickpocket, Procès de Jeanne d'Arc, Au Hasard
Balthazar, Mouchette, Une Femme douce,
Quatre nuits d'un rêveur.*

Above: Jean-Claude Brialy in LE BAL DU COMTE D'ORGEL. At right: Jean-Claude Brialy

82 BRIALY, Jean-Claude (1933 –). B: Aumale, Algeria. Actor, who can be dazzlingly funny when given the opportunity. Made his name thanks to the *Nouvelle Vague*.

Main films: *Le Coup du berger* (short), *Ascenseur pour l'échafaud, Le beau Serge, Les Cousins, Les 400 coups, Paris nous appartient, Le bel âge, Cléo de 5 à 7, Une Femme est une femme, Education sentimentale, Château en Suède, La Ronde* (64), *Un Homme de trop, Lamiel, La Mariée était en noir, Le Bal du Comte d'Orgel, Le Genou de Claire.*

83 BRION, Françoise (1934–). B: Paris. Stage and screen actress, with an enigmatic and intellectual appeal, much favoured by *Nouvelle Vague* directors.

Main films: *Le bel âge, L'Eau à la bouche, Le Cœur battant, La Dénonciation, L'Immortelle, Et Satan conduit le bal, Vacances portugaises, Codine, Dragées au poivre, Alexandre le bienheureux, Traité du rossignol, Un beau monstre.*

84 BROCA, Philippe de (1933–). B: Paris. Director. At first assistant. A specialist in light comedy, often using scripts by Daniel Boulanger (q.v.).

Films (also co-scripted): *Les Jeux de l'amour, Le Farceur, L'Amant de cinq jours, Cartouche, Les sept péchés capitaux* (one episode), *L'Homme de Rio, Un Monsieur de compagnie, Les Tribulations d'un Chinois en Chine, Le Roi de cœur, Le plus vieux métier du monde* (one episode), *Le Diable par la queue, Les Caprices de Marie, Le Cinéma de Papa* (acted only), *La Poudre d'escampette.*

85 BRUNIUS, Jacques-Bernard (1906– 1967). B: Paris. Journalist, writer, actor, and director. At first assistant to Clair, Buñuel etc. An unusual and gifted figure who wrote and directed some fifteen shorts, including *Violons d'Ingres* (37). Acted in several films, including *L'Age d'or, L'Affaire est dans le sac, Le Crime de M. Lange, Une Partie de campagne.* Brunius published a lively book of reminiscences: "En marge du cinéma français" (54).

86 BUÑUEL, Luis (1900–). B: Calanda. Great Spanish director, whose international career began in France, where he was to make some of his most important films.

Films (in France): *Un Chien Andalou, L'Age d'or, Cela s'appelle l'aurore, La Mort en ce jardin, La Fièvre monte à El Pao, Le Journal d'une femme de chambre, Belle de jour, La Voie lactée.*

Above: Luis Buñuel

87 BUREL, Léonce-Henry (1892–). B: Indret. Director of photography, at his peak during the Thirties and Forties. Worked with Abel Gance (q.v.) on several technical innovations.

Main films: *Mater dolorosa, La dixième symphonie, J'accuse, La Roue, Crainquebille, Visages d'enfants, Napoléon* (co., 27), *Boudu sauvé des eaux, La Mort du cygne, Journal d'un curé de campagne, La Vérité sur Bébé Donge, Un Condamné à mort s'est échappé, Pickpocket, Procès de Jeanne d'Arc.*

88 BUSSIÈRES, Raymond (1907–). B: Ivry-la-Bataille. Actor. At first appeared in cabaret and theatre. A specialist (alongside his wife) in witty Parisian roles.

Main films: *Nous les gosses, L'Assassin habite au 21, Les Portes de la nuit, Quai des Orfèvres, Justice est faite, Casque d'or, Porte des Lilas.*

89 CAMÉRA-STYLO. A phrase first coined in 1948, in *L'Ecran français*, by the director Alexandre Astruc (q.v.), as a definition of what he regarded as the fundamental characteristic of the new film language then in the process of development.

Under the title *Naissance d'une nouvelle avant-garde: la caméra-stylo*, Astruc wrote: "The cinema is becoming a means of expression like the other arts before it, especially painting and the novel. It is no longer a spectacle, a diversion equivalent to the old boulevard theatre, just the means of preserving the events of an era; it is becoming, little by little, a visual language, i.e. a medium in which and by which an artist can express his thoughts, be they abstract or whatever, or in which he can communicate his obsessions as accurately as he can do today in an essay or a novel. That is why I call this new age of the cinema that of the *caméra-stylo*."

Direction therefore becomes a form of writing, and films should be written (scripted) and shot by the same person; thus we have the origins of the *auteur* theory. These ideas, which were at the root of the thinking of the future *Nouvelle Vague* (q.v.), have been upheld in the magazines *La Revue du Cinéma* (1946 – 49), and then in *Cahiers du Cinéma* (from 1951).

90 CAMUS, Marcel (1912 –). B: Chappes. Director. At first assistant to Feyder, Becker, Buñuel, and others. A competent but rather colourless film-maker, whose reputation rests on the award-winning *Orfeu negro*.

Films (also scripted or co-scripted): *Mort en fraude, Orfeu negro, Os Bandeirantes, L'Oiseau de paradis, Le Chant du monde, Vivre la nuit, Le Temps fou, Le Mur de l'Atlantique*.

At right: Marcel Camus

91 CANTAGREL, Marc (1879 – 1960). B. and D: Paris. Chemical engineer, and a pioneer of scientific and educational cinema in France. Directed several such films, including *La Bière, La Métallurgie, Le Gyroscope, La Force centrifuge, L'Organisation scientifique du travail, Familles de droites et de paraboles, Lieux géométriques*.

92 CANUDO, Ricciotto (1879 – 1923). B: Italy. D: Paris. Critic and aesthete, connected with the *futuriste* group and with *avant-garde* circles. He lived in Paris and wrote in French. One of the first film theorists, he termed the cinema "the Seventh Art." His writings on film were published as "L'Usine aux images" (27).

93 CAPELLANI, Albert (1870 – 1931). B. and D: Paris. An important director of the period 1910 – 20, famous for his excellent screen versions of literary classics.

Main films: *L'Assommoir, Les deux orphelines, Notre-Dame de Paris* (11), *Le Roman d'un jeune homme pauvre, Les Misérables, Les*

Mystères de Paris, Germinal (13), *Quatre-vingt-treize.*

94 CARBONNAUX, Norbert (1918–).
B: Neuilly. Director. At first scriptwriter and dialogue writer. Some of his work helped to revive French film comedy during the Fifties.

Films: *Les Corsaires du Bois de Boulogne, Courte tête, Le Temps des œufs durs, Candide, La Gamberge, Toutes folles de lui.*

95 CARETTE, Julien (1897–1966). B: Paris. D: Vésinet. Stage and screen actor. At first appeared in music hall and revues. Always lively and amusing, best remembered for his supporting roles as the "common man."

Main films: *L'Affaire est dans le sac, La grande illusion, Entrée des artistes, La Marseillaise, La Bête humaine, La Règle du jeu, Les Portes de la nuit, Occupe-toi d'Amélie, L'Auberge rouge, Le Joueur, La Jument verte, L'Amour d'une femme, Les Aventures de Salavin, Pantalaskas.*

96 CARNÉ, Marcel (1909–). B: Paris. Major director during the "poetic realism" phase of French cinema. After being a journalist and critic, he caused a stir with his first short, very much in the impressionist style—*Nogent, Eldorado du Dimanche* (29). From 1930–35: assisted Clair and Feyder (qq.v.). His best work was done between 1935 and 1945, largely due to his collaboration with Jacques Prévert (q.v.).

Films (also co-scripted*): *Jenny, Drôle de drame, Quai des brumes, Hôtel du Nord, Le Jour se lève, Les Visiteurs du soir, Les Enfants du paradis, Les Portes de la nuit, La Marie du port*, Juliette ou la clef des songes, Thérèse Raquin*, L'Air de Paris, Le Pays d'où je viens, Les Tricheurs*, Terrain vague*, Du Mouron pour les petits oiseaux, Trois chambres à Manhattan*, Les jeunes loups*, La Force et le droit*.*

97 CAROL, Martine (1922–1967). B: Biarritz. D: Monte Carlo. Actress. The top French film star during the Fifties. Her somewhat statuesque beauty was offset by a Gallic coquettishness that served her best in *Caroline chérie.*

Main films: *Voyage surprise, Les Amants de Vérone, Caroline chérie, Belles de Nuit, La Spiaggia* (Lattuada, Italy, 53), *Lola Montès, Austerlitz, Nathalie agent secret, Vanina Vanini* (Rossellini, Italy, 61).

98 CARRIÈRE, Jean-Claude (1931–). Highly respected and versatile scriptwriter, a regular collaborator of Pierre Etaix's and Buñuel's (qq.v.).

Photo LIMOT

Above: Marcel Carné. Opposite: Carné's
LES VISITEURS DU SOIR

Films (main shorts): *Rupture, Heureux anniversaire, Insomnie, La Pince à ongles*. Features: *Le Soupirant, Le Journal d'une femme de chambre, Yoyo, Viva Maria, Tant qu'on a la santé, Belle de jour, La Voie lactée* (also acted), *Le grand amour, La Piscine, Borsalino* (co.), *L'Alliance* (also acted), *Sérieux comme le plaisir* (co. Benayoun).

99 CASARÈS, Maria (1922 –   ). Stage and screen actress, born in Spain. She has played a number of tragic parts, projecting an extraordinary emotional power despite her restrained appearance. Her spell with Gérard Philipe (q.v.) at the TNP produced several memorable productions.

Main films: *Les Enfants du paradis, Les Dames du Bois de Boulogne, La septième porte, La Chartreuse de Parme, Orphée, Le Testament d'Orphée*.

100 CASSEL, Jean-Pierre (1932 –   ). B: Paris. Stage and screen actor, whose humour and gaiety makes him ideally suited to comedy roles.

Main films: *En cas de malheur, Les Jeux de l'amour, Le Farceur, Candide, L'Amant de cinq jours, Les sept péchés capitaux, Cyrano et d'Artagnan, Le Caporal épinglé, Un Monsieur de compagnie, Paris brûle-t-il?, Jeu de massacre, Les Femmes, L'Ours et la poupée, L'Armée des ombres, La Rupture, Le Bateau*.

101 CAVALCANTI, Alberto (1897 –   ). B: Rio de Janeiro. Director. Began his career in France, where he was involved with the *impressionist avant-garde*, and then worked in England, Germany, and Italy. After the Second World War he returned briefly to Brazil to help build up the country's cinema. Cavalcanti began as a set designer (*L'Inhumaine, Feu Mathias Pascal* etc.) and was assistant to Marcel L'Herbier (q.v.) between 1922 and 1925.

Main films (in France; also scripted*): *Rien que les heures**, *Yvette** (also art direction), *En rade**, *Le Train sans yeux**, *Le Capitaine Fracasse, Le petit chaperon rouge**, *La petite Lili**.

102 CAVALIER, Alain (1931 –   ). B: Vendôme. Director. At first film school and then assistant to Louis Malle (q.v.). He has managed to assert his talent in only a handful of films. Also co-scripted *La Vie de château*. Short: *Un Américain* (58).

Films: *Le Combat dans l'île, L'Insoumis, Mise à sac, La Chamade*.

103 CAYATTE, André (1909 –   ). B: Carcassonne. Director. At first lawyer, journalist, and writer; then scriptwriter (on *Entrée des artistes, Remorques*). A film-maker who regards the cinema as a didactic medium and whose films on the problems of justice are his most solid and best known.

Films: *La fausse maîtresse, Au Bonheur des dames, Pierre et Jean, Le dernier sou, Sérénade aux nuages, Roger la honte, La Revanche de Roger la honte, Le Chanteur inconnu, Le Dessous des cartes, Les Amants de Vérone, Retour à la vie* (one episode), *Justice est faite, Nous sommes tous des assassins, Avant le déluge, Le Dossier noir, Œil pour œil, Le Miroir à deux faces, Le Passage du Rhin, Le Glaive et la balance, La Vie conjugale* (two parts: *Jean-Marc* and *Françoise*), *Piège pour Cendrillon, Les Risques du métier, Les Chemins de Katmandou, Mourir d'aimer*.

104 CAYROL, Jean (1911 –   ). B: Bordeaux. Writer and scriptwriter (*Muriel*), who also wrote the commentary for *Nuit et brouillard*. In collaboration with Claude Durand, he made a series of distinguished shorts, including *On vous parle* (60), *La Frontière* (61), *Madame se meurt* (62). Feature: *Le Coup de grâce* (co. Claude Durand). Author (also with Durand) of an interesting essay on film, "Le Droit de regard" (63).

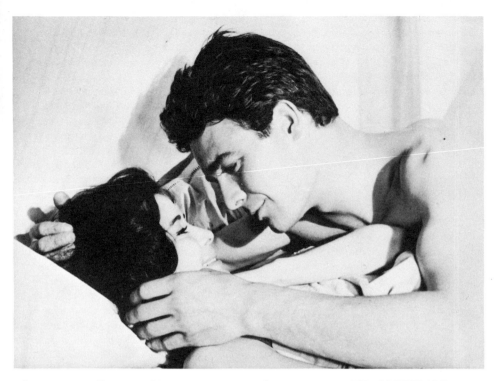

Above: Jacques Charrier and Marie-José Nat in André Cayatte's LA VIE CONJUGALE.
Below: Claude Chabrol

105 C H A B R O L, Claude (1930 –   ). B: Paris. Director. At first critic (a book on Hitchcock with Eric Rohmer, q.v.). One of the true "creators" of the *Nouvelle Vague* (he produced his first film entirely by himself), Chabrol's flair for social satire and his all-pervasive black humour have developed richly during the past decade. Acted: *Le Coup du berger, Les Jeux de l'amour, L'Eau à la bouche, Saint Tropez Blues, Paris nous appartient.*

Films (also acted * and/or co-scripted †): *Le beau Serge*†, *Les Cousins†, A double tour, Les bonnes femmes, Les Godelureaux†, Les sept péchés capitaux* (one episode), *L'Œil du malin†, Ophélia†, Landru*, Les plus belles escroqueries du monde* (one episode), *Le Tigre aime la chair*

fraîche, *Marie-Chantal contre le Dr Kah**†, *Paris vu par . . .**† (one episode), *La Ligne de démarcation**†, *Le Tigre se parfume à la dynamite*, *Le Scandale*†, *La Route de Corinthe*, *Les Biches*†, *La Femme infidèle*†, *Que la bête meure*, *Le Boucher*†, *Le Rupture*†, *Juste avant la nuit*†.

106 CHALONGE, Christian de (1937 –). B: Douai. Director. At first assistant to Verneuil, Clouzot, Franju etc. Began his career with a brave film, *O Salto*. Has since made *L'Alliance*.

107 CHAPIER, Henri (1931 –). Film critic of the newspaper *Combat*, who has campaigned passionately for the so-called "new cinema." He turned to direction with *Sierra Falcon* (short doc., 67) and *Un Eté américain* (medium-length doc., 68), and has worked in TV.

Films: *Sex Power, Les Collines de Sion.*

108 CHARRIER, Jacques (1936 –). B: Metz. Actor. One of the "jeune premiers" of the *Nouvelle Vague*.

Main films: *Les Tricheurs, Les Dragueurs, Babette s'en va-t-en guerre, L'Œil du malin; A cause, à cause d'une femme; La Vie conjugale, Marie-Soleil, Les Créatures, Money Money, Sirocco* (Jancsó, Hungary, 69).

109 CHAVANCE, Louis (1907 –). B: Paris. Scriptwriter and dialogue writer. At first journalist and assistant, he became well-known during the Forties.

Main films: *La Nuit fantastique, Dernier atout, Le Corbeau, Un Revenant, La Marie du port.*

110 CHENAL, Pierre (1904 –). B: Brussels. Director of modest ability who nevertheless was quite important in the Thirties. 1942 – 44: lived in Argentina.

Main films: *Crime et châtiment* (34), *Les Mutinés de l'Elseneur, L'Homme de nulle part, La Maison du Maltais, Alibi, Le dernier tournant, La Foire aux chimères, Clochemerle.*

111 CHEVALIER, Maurice (1887 –). B: Paris. Famous actor on both stage and screen, and equally well-loved as a singer and music hall artiste. 1911 – 14: acted in shorts by Max Linder (q.v.).

Main films: *The Love Parade* (Lubitsch, U.S.A., 29), *The Smiling Lieutenant* (Lubitsch, U.S.A., 31), *Love Me Tonight* (Mamoulian, U.S.A., 32), *The Merry Widow* (Lubitsch, U.S.A., 34), *Fausses nouvelles, Pièges* (Siodmak, France, 39), *Le Silence est d'or, Love in the Afternoon* (Wilder, U.S.A., 57), *Gigi* (Minnelli, U.S.A., 58), *Fanny* (Logan, U.S.A., 61).

112 CHOMETTE, Henri (1895 – 1941). B. and D: Rabat. Director. Brother of René CLAIR. Made several *avant-garde* shorts: *Jeux des reflets et de la vitesse, Cinq minutes de cinéma pur, A quoi rêvent les jeunes filles* (23 – 25). His later feature films were uninteresting.

113 CHRÉTIEN, Henri (1879 – 1956). B: Paris. D: Washington. In 1927 he invented a special lens named *hypergonar*, one of the antecedents of the CinemaScope process. His patent was ignored in France save for Autant-Lara's *Construire un feu* (28), but was bought by Fox in 1952 and put to commercial use.

114 CHRISTIAN-JAQUE (1904 –). B: Paris. RN: Christian Maudet. A prolific and interesting director. At first journalist, poster designer, and assistant to Duvivier (q.v.).

Main films: *François Ier, Les Perles de la couronne* (co. Guitry), *Les Pirates du rail, Les Disparus de Saint-Agil, Premier bal, L'Assassinat du Père Noël, La Symphonie fantastique, Carmen, Sortilèges, Boule de suif, Un Revenant, La Chartreuse de Parme, Souvenirs perdus,*

Above: Maurice Chevalier in LE SILENCE EST D'OR. Below: Christian-Jaque

Fanfan la Tulipe, Nana (55), *Si tous les gars du monde, Babette s'en va-t-en guerre, La Tulipe noire, Les bonnes causes, Les Amours de Lady Hamilton.*

115 CIAMPI, Yves (1921 –   ). B: Paris. An original and appealing director. At first assistant.

Main films: *Un grand patron, Les Héros sont fatigués, Typhon sur Nagasaki, Qui êtes-vous M. Sorge?, Liberté I, Le Ciel sur la tête, A quelques jours près.*

116 CINÉMATHÈQUE FRANÇAISE. Archive organisation for the preservation and screening of films, founded in 1936 by Henri

Langlois (with the collaboration of Georges Franju and Jean Mitry). Since then it has rescued tens of thousands of old films and has arranged numerous daily showings for the public. Henri Langlois continues to be the Secretary-General, after a brief departure during the "affair" in which the French government involved him in April 1968.

117 CINÉMA-VÉRITÉ. A term, or rather formula, introduced in 1961 by the makers of *Chronique d'un été*. It is a literal translation of the Russian term *kino pravda*, which was generally used to describe the kind of film-making practised in the U.S.S.R. during the Twenties by Dziga Vertov, the champion of *kino-glaz* ("film eye"); in other words, improvised shooting free of rigid direction (if not of careful editing). Influenced by TV and the methods of the *Nouvelle Vague*, the makers of *Chronique d'un été* (Jean Rouch and Edgar Morin) attempted to catch the essential truth of events and people's lives by filming them directly. This brand of *cinéma direct* had already been put to the test earlier in England (*free cinema*) and in Canada by a number of documentarists. The term *candid camera* is sometimes referred to, although *cinéma-vérité* is understood everywhere.

118 CLAIR, René (1898–). B: Paris. RN: René Chomette. Important and much revered director. At first journalist, actor (*Parisette* and *Orpheline* series), and assistant to Feuillade (q.v.). 1935–1938: lives in Britain. 1940: to U.S.A. 1946: returns to France. Clair formed his style midway between impressionism and realism, creating a picturesque world from the crowded *quartiers* of his native Paris. The structure of his films is based largely on the almost balletic movement of the characters as they give chase to one another or to their objective. Clair scripted *Prix de beauté* (Genina, 29) and all his own films except*.

Films: *Paris qui dort, Entracte*, Le Fantôme du Moulin Rouge, Le Voyage imaginaire, La Proie du vent, Un Chapeau de paille d'Italie, La Tour* (short, 24), *Les deux timides, Sous les toits de Paris, Le Million, A nous la liberté, Quatorze Juillet, Le dernier milliardaire*. In Britain: *The Ghost Goes West, Break the News*. In France: *Air pur* (unfinished). In U.S.A.: *The Flame of New Orleans, Forever and a Day* (one episode, 42), *I Married a Witch* (42), *It Happened Tomorrow* (43), *And Then There Were None/Ten Little Niggers* (45). In France: *Le Silence est d'or, La Beauté du diable, Les Belles de nuit, Les grandes manœuvres, Porte des Lilas, La Française et l'amour* (one episode), *Tout l'or du monde, Les quatre vérités* (one episode), *Les Fêtes galantes*.

119 CLÉMENT, René (1913–). B: Bordeaux. Major director whose work often has an objective rigour as well as a moral and psychological strength. At first several shorts, including *Soigne ton gauche* (36, *début* of Jacques Tati, q.v.), *Ceux du rail* (42), and *La grande pastorale* (43).

Films (also co-scripted *): *La Bataille du rail, La Belle et la bête* (technical adviser to Cocteau), *Le Père tranquille, Les Maudits, Au-delà des grilles, Le Château de verre, Jeux interdits*, Monsieur Ripois** (shot in Britain), *Gervaise, Barrage contre le Pacifique*, Plein soleil*, Quelle joie de vivre** (shot in Italy), *Le Jour et l'heure*, Les Félins*, Paris brûle-t-il?, Le Passager de la pluie La Maison sous les arbres.*

120 CLÉMENTI, Pierre (1942 –   ). B: Paris. Stage and screen actor, noted for his fierce and temperamental roles. An active member of the underground film movement. Directed two "underground style" shorts: *Visa de Censure No. X* (67) and *Carte de Voeux* (69).

Main films: *Il gattopardo* (Visconti, Italy, 63), *Les Iles enchantées, Un Homme de trop,* *Lamiel, Belle de jour, Benjamin, Partner* (Berto-lucci, Italy, 68), *La Voie lactée, Antenna* (Ditvoorst, Netherlands, 69), *Porcile* (Pasolini, Italy, 69), *I cannibali* (Cavani, Italy, 70), *Jupiter, Blanche.*

121 CLOCHE, Maurice (1907 –   ). B: Commercy. Prolific director who has rarely concerned himself with social or psychological problems.

Main films: *Monsieur Vincent, Docteur Laënnec, La Cage aux filles, Prisons de femmes, Un Missionaire, La Porteuse de pain, Requiem pour un caïd.*

122 CLOÉREC, René (1911 –   ). B: Paris. Composer, whose music and songs have had quality as well as popular appeal. He has

Pierre Clémenti and Catherine Deneuve in BENJAMIN

Pierre Fresnay, Ginette Leclerc and Bernard Lancret in Clouzot's LE CORBEAU

scored most of Autant-Lara's (q.v.) films since *Douce*. Other scores: *La Cage aux rossignols, Le Père tranquille, Premières armes, Châteaux en Espagne* etc.

123 CLOQUET, Ghislain (1924 –). B: Antwerp. Director of photography. A leading figure in the *Nouvelle Vague*. 1946 – 47: studied at IDHEC, then assistant to Edmond Séchan (q.v.). Various medium-length films including *Les Statues meurent aussi, Toute la mémoire du monde,* and *Nuit et brouillard* (all dir. Resnais).

Main films: *Un Amour de poche, Le bel âge, La belle Américaine, Classe tous risques, Le Trou, Les Honneurs de la guerre, Un nommé La Rocca, Le Feu follet, Mickey One* (Penn, U.S.A., 64), *Au hasard Balthazar, Les Demoiselles de Rochefort*. In Belgium: *The Man Who Had His Hair Cut Short* (Delvaux, 66), and

Un Soir un train (Delvaux, 67). In France: *Mouchette, Benjamin, Mazel Tov ou le Mariage, Une Femme douce, La Maison des Bories, La Décharge, Peau d'âne*.

124 CLOUZOT, Henri-Georges (1907 –). B: Niort. Leading director, respected for his naturalistic style and his flair for suspense. Studied political science, then became film critic (1928 – 30). Scriptwriter on a dozen films between 1931 and 1941, including *Le Dernier des six, Les Inconnus dans la maison*.

Films (also co-scripted *): *L'Assassin habite au 21, Le Corbeau, Quai des Orfèvres, Manon, Retour à la vie* (one episode), *Miquette et sa mère, Le Salaire de la peur*, Les Diaboliques*, Le Mystère Picasso* (also acted), *Les Espions*, La Vérité*, La Prisonnière**.

125 COCTEAU, Jean (1889 – 1963). B: Maisons-Laffitte. D: Milly-la-Forêt. A renowned and in many ways unique personality in the French cultural world. Scripted and wrote dialogue for all his own films and *La Comédie du bonheur, Le Baron fantôme, Les Dames du Bois de Boulogne, Ruy Blas, La Voix humaine* (*L'Amore,* Rossellini, 48), *Les Enfants terribles, La Princesse de Clèves.* As a director, Cocteau was much influenced by *surrealism* (q.v.).

Films as director: *Le Sang d'un poète, L'éternel retour* (co. Delannoy), *La Belle et la bête* (co. Clément), *L'Aigle à deux têtes, Les Parents terribles, Orphée, Coriolan* (short, 50), *Villa Santo Sospir* (short, 51), *Le Testament d'Orphée.*

126 COGGIO, Roger (1934 –   ). B: Lyon. Stage and screen actor; also director.

Main films: *Avant le déluge, Les Fruits de l'été, Pardonnez-nous nos offenses, Soledad, Une Histoire immortelle.* As director: *Le Journal d'un fou* (scripted from Gogol, and acted), *Chronique d'un couple.*

127 COHL, Émile (1857 – 1938). B: Paris. D: Orly. RN: Emile Courtet. Designer and cartoonist. One of the earliest and most illustrious pioneers of *animation* (q.v.). Specialised in creating funny little figures that could undergo innumerable transformations, notably in the *Fantoches* series. 1912 – 14: to U.S.A. Between 1908 and 1918 Cohl produced about a hundred cartoons, including *Fantasmagorie,*

Edouard Dermit and Jean Cocteau in the latter's LE TESTAMENT D'ORPHÉE

Cauchemar du Fantoche, Drame chez les Fantoches, Les joyeux microbes, Les Lunettes fééri-ques, Le tout petit Faust (puppets), *Les Jouets animés, L'Homme sans tête, Le Baron de Crac, Les Aventures des Pieds Nickelés* (series co. dir. B. Rabier).

128 C O L P I, Henri (1921 –   ). B: Brigue, Switzerland. Director and editor. Main films as editor: *La Pointe courte, Nuit et brouillard, Le Mystère Picasso, A King in New York* (Chaplin, 57), *Hiroshima mon amour, L'Année dernière à Marienbad, Concerto pour un exil* (Ecaré, 67). Colpi has proved himself an original and engaging director, and has also written a useful critical dictionary, "Le Cinéma et ses hommes" (47) as well as the standard work in French on film music, "Défense et illustration de la musique dans le film" (62).

Films (also scripted): *Une aussi longue absence, Codine, Mona l'étoile sans nom, Heureux qui comme Ulysse*. Also TV series.

129 C O M P A N E E Z, Jacques (1906 – 1956). B: Russia. D: Paris. Prolific scriptwriter, who handled the scenario for several successful films.

Main films: *Les Bas-fonds, La Maison du Maltais, L'inévitable M. Dubois, Les Maudits, Copie conforme, Souvenirs perdus, Casque d'Or.*

C O M P A N E E Z, Nina (1938 –   ). B: Paris. His daughter. Has co-scripted all the films directed by her husband, Michel Deville (q.v.).

C O S T A - G A V R A S *see* **G A V R A S, Costa.**

Michel Cournot and Annie Girardot in LES GAULOISES BLEUES

Raoul Coutard directing HOA-BINH

130 COURCEL, Nicole (1930–). B: Saint-Cloud. Lively and talented actress.

Main films: *Rendez-vous de Juillet, La Marie du port, Les Amants de Bras-Mort, La Sorcière, Le Passage du Rhin, Les Dimanches de Ville-d'Avray, L'Etrangleur.*

131 COURNOT, Michel (1922–). Director. At first novelist, journalist, and then a controversial and enthusiastic film critic.

Film: *Les Gauloises bleues,* a bitter and violent criticism of society.

132 COUSTEAU, Jacques-Yves (1910–). B: Saint-André. Famous underwater scientist and explorer, who has made several short films on the subject, including *Epaves* (45), *Paysages du silence* (47), *Autour d'un récif* (48), *Carnet de plongée* (50), and TV series.

Features (also scripted and photographed): *Le Monde du silence* (co. Louis Malle), *Le Monde sans soleil.*

133 COUTANT, André (1906–). Manufacturer of film equipment. He launched the well-known *Eclair 16 Coutant* camera—light, manoeuvrable, silent, and practical—which during the past decade has facilitated the shooting of "direct" cinema and has exerted a considerable influence on the aesthetics of "new cinema" and *cinéma-vérité* throughout the world.

134 COUTARD, Raoul (1924–). B: Paris. Director of photography. Thanks to his training as a press photographer (*Paris-Match, Life,* etc.) and newsreel cameraman, Coutard helped to define the aesthetic attitudes of the

Nouvelle Vague, especially in the films of Godard *.

Main films: *A bout de souffle*, Tirez sur le pianiste, Le petit soldat*, Lola, Chronique d'un été* (co.), *Une Femme est une femme*, Jules et Jim, La Poupée, Vivre sa vie*, Les Carabiniers*, Le Mépris*, Vacances portugaises, Et Satan conduit le bal, La Peau douce, Bande à part*, Une Femme mariée*, Un Monsieur de compagnie, La 317ème Section, Alphaville*, Pierrot le fou*, Deux ou trois choses que je sais d'elle*, Made in USA*, L'Horizon, La Chinoise*, Week-end*, La Mariée était en noir, Z, L'Aveu, La Liberté en croupe, L'Explosion.* As director: *Hoa-Binh.*

135   CRAVENNE, Marcel (1908–). Director. At first assistant. Made one notable film (from the Strindberg play): *La Danse de mort.*

136   CUNY, Alain (1913–). B: Saint Malo. Stage and screen actor, usually playing romantic and, in more recent years, dramatic roles. Often seen in major Italian productions.

Main films: *Les Visiteurs du soir, Le Baron fantôme, Cristo proibito* (Malaparte, Italy, 50), *Mina de Vanghel, La Signora senza camelie* (Antonioni, Italy, 53), *Les Amants, La dolce vita* (Fellini, Italy, 59), *Fellini-Satyricon* (Fellini, Italy, 69), *Uomini contro* (Rosi, Italy, 70); *Valparaiso, Valparaiso.*

137   DALIO, Marcel (1900–). B: Paris. Actor, whose appealing personality made him a successful "Frenchman" in many American productions.

Main films: *Pépé le Moko, Un grand amour de Beethoven, La grande illusion, Les Perles de la couronne, Entrée des artistes, La Maison du Maltais, La Règle du jeu, The Shanghai Gesture* (Sternberg, U.S.A., 41), *To Have and Have Not* (Hawks, U.S.A., 45), *Les Maudits, Dédée d'Anvers, Les Amants de Vérone, Snows of Kilimanjaro* (King, U.S.A., 52), *Razzia sur la chnouf, Sabrina* (Wilder, U.S.A., 54), *The Sun Also Rises* (King, U.S.A., 57), *Classe tous risques, Cancan* (Walter Lang, U.S.A., 59), *Cartouche, Le Monocle rit jaune, Un Monsieur de compagnie, Catch 22* (Nichols, U.S.A., 70).

138   DAQUIN, Louis (1908–). B: Calais. Director. At first journalist and assistant. His films usually adopt a progressive approach to social and human problems.

Films: *Nous les gosses, Madame et le mort, Le Voyageur de la Toussaint, Premier de cordée, Patrie, Les Frères Bouquinquant, Le Point du jour, Le Parfum de la dame en noir, Maître après Dieu, Bel-Ami, Les Chardons du Baragan, Les Arrivistes, La Foire aux cancres.* Daquin has also written an interesting book based on his experiences as a film-maker: "Le Cinéma, notre métier" (60).

139   DARC, Mireille (1938–). B: Toulon. Actress who has become a star thanks to her vitality and comedy flair. Also stage work.

Main films: *La Bride sur le cou, Les nouveaux*

aristocrates, Monsieur, Les Barbouzes, Galia, La grande sauterelle, Week-end, Jeff, Madly, Fantasia chez les ploucs; Laisse aller, c'est une valse.

140 DARRIEUX, Danielle (1917 –   ). B: Bordeaux. Actress. At first studied music. A major star, in theatre as well as cinema, during the Forties, and still as elegant as ever in recent screen appearances. 1970: acted in *Coco* on Broadway.

Main films: *Mayerling, Battements de cœur, Premier rendez-vous, Ruy Blas, Occupe-toi d'Amélie, La Ronde, Five Fingers* (Mankiewicz, U.S.A., 52), *Le Plaisir, La Vérité sur Bébé Donge, Le bon dieu sans confession, Madame de . . ., Le Rouge et le noir, Napoléon, Le Salaire du péché, Les Yeux de l'amour, Si Paris nous était conté, Pot-Bouille, Marie-Octobre, Landru, Le Coup de grâce, Les Demoiselles de*

Rochefort, Le Dimanche de la vie, Les Oiseaux vont mourir au Pérou, 24h. de la vie d'une femme.

141 DAUPHIN, Claude (1903 –   ). B: Corbeil. Stage and screen actor.

Main films: *Entrée des artistes, Battements de cœur, Une Femme disparaît, Le Plaisir, Casque d'or* (his best part), *Les mauvaises rencontres, The Quiet American* (Mankiewicz, U.S.A., 57), *Symphonie pour un massacre, Paris brûle-t-il?, Lady L* (Ustinov, U.S.A., 65), *Lamiel, L'Une et l'autre, Barbarella, Hard Contract* (Pogostin, U.S.A., 68), *The Madwoman of Chaillot* (Forbes, Britain, 69).

142 DEBRIE, André (1891 – 1967). B. and D: Paris. Famous inventor and engineer. Main inventions: the Parvo camera, still in use today (1908); an automatic developer (1925); Truca apparatus (1936). Helped Abel Gance (q.v.) to develop the triple screen, predecessor of Cinerama.

143 DECAË, Henri (1915 –   ). B: Saint-Denis. Brilliant director of photography, closely associated with the *Nouvelle Vague*. An

expert at handling colour. Photographed nearly fifty shorts.

Main films: *Le Silence de la mer, Les Enfants terribles, Bob le flambeur, S.O.S. Noronha, Ascenseur pour l'échafaud, Le beau Serge, Les Amants, Les Cousins, Les 400 coups, La Sentence, A double tour, Les bonnes femmes, Plein soleil, Quelle joie de vivre, Léon Morin, prêtre; Vie privée, Les Dimanches de Ville-d'Avray, L'Aîné des Ferchaux, Le Jour et l'heure, Dragées au poivre, La Tulipe noire, Les Félins, La Ronde* (64), *Week-end à Zuydcoote, Le Corniaud, Viva Maria, Le Voleur, The Comedians* (Glenville, U.S.A., 67), *Diaboliquement vôtre, Le Samouraï, Le Clan des Siciliens, The Only Game in Town* (Stevens, U.S.A., 69), *Le Cercle rouge, La Folie des grandeurs.*

144 DECOIN, Henri (1896 – 1969). B: Paris. Director. At first journalist. 1929 – 32: assistant and scriptwriter. Several solid commercial productions.

Main films: *Abus de confiance, Battements de cœur, Premier rendez-vous, Les Inconnus dans*

la maison, Les Amoureux sont seuls au monde, La Vérité sur Bébé Donge, Razzia sur la chnouf, Nathalie agent secret, Le Pavé de Paris, Les Parias de la gloire.*

145 DELANNOY, Jean (1908 –). B: Noisy-le-Sec. Director. At first editor and assistant (from 1927). Prolific but mediocre, at his most ambitious during the Forties.

Main films: *Paris Deauville, Macao l'enfer du jeu, Pontcarral, L'éternel retour, La Symphonie pastorale, Les Jeux sont faits, Aux Yeux du souvenir, Dieu a besoin des hommes, Le Garçon sauvage, La Minute de vérité, Notre-Dame de Paris, Maigret tend un piège, Le Baron de l'Ecluse, La Princesse de Clèves, Les Amitiés particulières, Le Soleil des voyous, La Peau de torpedo.*

146 DELERUE, Georges (1925 –). B: Roubaix. Composer, also conductor. At first cinema commercials and shorts (including *La première nuit, Du Côté de la côte, Le Sourire, Les Marines, Opéra mouffe, Le Bureau des mariages, A*). Came to prominence due to his lyrical, wistful, often gay scores for *Nouvelle Vague* directors.

Main films: *Le bel âge, Hiroshima mon amour* (waltz only), *Les Jeux de l'amour, Une Fille pour l'été, Classe tous risques, Le Farceur, La Morte-saison des amours, L'Amant de cinq jours, Tirez sur le pianiste, Une aussi longue absence, Cartouche, Jules et Jim, La Dénonciation, L'Immortelle, Les Tontons flingueurs, Le Meurtrier, Vacances portugaises, Le Mépris, L'Aîné des Ferchaux, L'Insoumis, L'Homme de Rio, La Peau douce, Un Monsieur de compagnie, The Pumpkin Eater* (Clayton, Britain, 64), *Mata Hari agent H-21, Viva Maria, Le Roi de cœur, Le vieil homme et l'enfant, Le Dimanche de la vie, A Man for All Seasons* (Zinnemann, Britain, 67), *Our Mother's House* (Clayton,

Above: Henri Decoin. Opposite: Henri Decaë at work on L'AÎNÉ DES FERCHAUX

Britain, 67), *Le Cerveau, Le Diable par la queue, La Promesse de l'aube* (Dassin, 70).

147 DELLUC, Louis (1890 – 1924). B: Cadouin. D: Paris. Critic, novelist, director. One of the pioneers of film criticism, founder of such specialised magazines as *Cinéa* (in 1921), and a promoter of the film society movement. As a theorist, he formulated an *impressionist* concept of cinema and emphasised the *magical* power of film imagery.

Main books: "Cinéma et Cie" (19), "Photogénie" (20), "Charlot" (21). As a director, Delluc was notable for his use of *avant-garde* methods.

Main films: *Fièvre, La Femme de nulle part, L'Inondation.* The "Prix Delluc" was established in 1937 to commemorate him, and has become an important and much respected award. Films that have won the "Prix Delluc" during recent years: *On n'enterre pas le dimanche, Une aussi longue absence, Un Cœur gros comme ça, Le Soupirant, L'Immortelle, Les Parapluies de Cherbourg, Le Bonheur, La Vie de château, La Guerre est finie, Benjamin, Baisers volés, Les Choses de la vie, Le Genou de Claire.*

148 DELON, Alain (1935 –). B: Sceaux. A leading box-office star for more than a decade, due mainly to his thrustful personality and dashing good looks. Since 1964: also producer, with his own company Adel. Several small parts before *Plein soleil.*

Main films: *Plein soleil, Rocco e i suoi fratelli* (Visconti, Italy, 60), *Quelle joie de vivre, L'eclisse* (Antonioni, Italy, 62), *Le Diable et les dix commandements, Il gattopardo* (Visconti, Italy, 63), *Mélodie en sous-sol, La Tulipe noire, Les Félins, L'Insoumis, The Yellow Rolls-Royce* (Asquith, Britain, 64), *Once a Thief* (Nelson, U.S.A., 65), *The Lost Command* (Robson, U.S.A., 65), *Paris brûle-t-il?, Texas across the River* (Gordon, U.S.A., 66), *Les Aventuriers, Histoires extraordinaires* (*William Wilson* episode), *Le Samouraï, Diaboliquement vôtre, The Girl on a Motorcycle* (Cardiff, Britain/France, 68), *Adieu l'ami, La Piscine, Jeff, Le Clan des Siciliens, Borsalino, Le Cercle rouge, Madly, Doucement les basses.*

149 DELOUCHE, Dominique (1931 –). B: Paris. Director. At first assistant to Fellini, then short films, including *Le Spectre de la danse* (60), *Portrait d'un violoncelle* (61), *La Messe sur le monde* (63), *Aquarelle* (65), *Avec Claude Monet* (66).

Films: *24h. de la vie d'une femme, L'Homme de désir.*

150 DEMY, Jacques (1931 –). B: Pont-Château. Director. 1949 – 51: studied at ENPC. At first assistant to Grimault and Rouquier (qq.v.). Then shorts: *Le Sabotier du Val de Loire* (56), *Le bel indifférent* (57), *Musée Grévin*

Above: Jacques Demy. Opposite: Alain Delon in MÉLODIE EN SOUS-SOL

(58), *La Mère et l'enfant* (59) (last two in collab. with Jean Masson), *Ars* (59). Married to Agnès VARDA (q.v.). Demy has created his own lyrical and romantic world, and has made a gallant attempt to establish the film musical in France.

Films (also scripted or co-scripted): *Lola, Les sept péchés capitaux* (one episode), *La Baie des Anges, Les Parapluies de Cherbourg, Les Demoiselles de Rochefort, Model Shop* (in U.S.A.), *Peau d'âne.*

151 D E N E U V E, Catherine (1943 –   ). B: Paris. RN: Catherine Dorléac. Highly talented actress, who has succeeded Brigitte Bardot these past few years as the main feminine attraction at the French box-office, thanks to her sincerity and fragile charm.

Main films: *Le Vice et la vertu, Et Satan conduit le bal, Vacances portugaises, Les plus belles escroqueries du monde, Les Parapluies de Cherbourg, Repulsion* (Polanski, Britain, 64), *La Vie de château, Le Chant du monde, Les Créatures, Les Demoiselles de Rochefort, Le Dimanche de la vie, Belle de jour, Benjamin, Manon 70, La Chamade, The April Fools* (Rosenberg, U.S.A., 68), *La Sirène du Mississipi, Tristana* (Buñuel, Spain/France, 69), *Peau d'âne, Ça n'arrive qu'aux autres.*

152 D E N N E R, Charles (1926 –   ). B: Tarnow, Poland. Stage and screen actor, with an unusual and forceful personality. 1946: stage *début*. Long spell at the TNP.

Main films: *La meilleure part, Ascenseur pour l'échafaud, Landru, La Vie à l'envers, Compartiment tueurs, Mata Hari agent H-21, Marie-Chantal contre le Dr. Kah, YUL 871* (Godbout, Canada, 66), *Le Voleur, La Mariée était en*

Opposite: Catherine Deneuve and Anne Vernon in LES PARAPLUIES DE CHERBOURG

noir, Le vieil homme et l'enfant, Z, La Trêve, Le Voyou.

153 D E R A Y, Jacques (1929 –   ). B: Lyon. Director. At first assistant. A sober, disciplined film-maker, whose work is always visually appealing.

Films: *Le Gigolo, Rififi à Tokyo, Symphonie pour un massacre, Par un beau matin d'été, Avec la peau des autres, L'Homme de Marrakech, La Piscine, Borsalino, Doucement les basses, Un peu de soleil dans l'eau froide.*

154 D E V I L L E, Michel (1931 –   ). B: Boulogne-sur-Seine. Director. At first assistant to Decoin (q.v.). In collaboration with his scriptwriter Nina Companeez, he has done wonders with the light comedy *genre* during the last few years.

Films (also co-scripted *): *Une Balle dans le canon* (co. dir. Charles Gérard), *Ce Soir ou jamais*, *Adorable menteuse* *; *A cause, à cause d'une femme* *; *L'Appartement des filles* *, Lucky*

Jo*, On a volé la Joconde*, Martin soldat, Benjamin ou les mémoires d'une puceau*; Bye bye, Barbara*; L'Ours et la poupée, Raphaël ou le débauché.

155 DEWEVER, Jean (1927 –   ). B: Paris. Director. At first assistant. Shorts include *La Crise du logement* (55). Features: *Les Honneurs de la guerre* (an engaging story about the Resistance), *César Grandblaise.*

156 DHÉRY, Robert (1921 –   ). B: Héry. RN: Robert Foulley. Circus performer, stage actor, and founder director of the comedy team known as the "Branquignols." His burlesque comedy style relies successfully on elaborate gags and hilarious situations. Acted in *Les Enfants du paradis, Sylvie et le fantôme* etc.

Films (as director): *Les Branquignols, Bertrand Cœur de Lion, La belle Américaine, Allez France!, Le petit baigneur.*

157 DIAMANT-BERGER,   Henri (1895 –   ). B: Paris. Critic, scriptwriter, producer, director. Established the magazine *Le Film* (1916 – 19). Has written several books, among them "Destin du cinéma français" (45). Founded the Association des Auteurs de

Alexandra Stewart and Jacques Doniol-Valcroze in LE BEL ÂGE

Films. A highly regarded figure in professional circles.

Main films: *Les trois mousquetaires, Education de prince, La Maternelle, Monsieur Fabre.* As producer only: *La belle Américaine.*

158 DONIOL-VALCROZE, Jacques (1920–). B: Paris. Journalist, critic, actor, novelist, and director. Chief Editor of *La Revue du Cinéma* (1946–49), then of *Cahiers du Cinéma* (1951–63). At first directed shorts. Acted in *Le bel âge, Vacances portugaises, L'Immortelle, Et Satan conduit le bal, Je t'aime, je t'aime, Le Voyou* etc. Doniol-Valcroze's interest has focused on erotic comedy and, more recently, on psychological thrillers.

Films (also scripted or co-scripted): *L'Eau à la bouche, Le Cœur battant, La Dénonciation, Le Viol, La Maison des Bories, L'Homme au cerveau greffé.*

159 DORLÉAC, Françoise (1942–1967). B: Paris. D: near Nice. An actress of considerable talent who was killed in a car accident. Sister of Catherine Deneuve (q.v.), her charm was at once elegant and vivacious.

Main films: *Ce soir ou jamais, Le Jeu de la vérité, La Gamberge, La Fille aux yeux d'or, Tout l'or du monde, Arsène Lupin contre Arsène Lupin, La Peau douce, L'Homme de Rio, Cul-de-Sac* (Polanski, Britain, 66), *Les Demoiselles de Rochefort, Billion Dollar Brain* (Russell, Britain, 67).

160 DOUY, Max (1914–). B: Issy-les-Moulineaux. Well-known set designer who has exerted a powerful influence on some of the best French films with his inventive but disciplined *décors*. Long association with Autant-Lara * (q.v.).

Main films: *Le Ciel est à vous, Les Dames du Bois de Boulogne, Falbalas, Le Diable au* corps*, *Quai des Orfèvres, Manon, Occupe-toi d'Amélie*, L'Auberge rouge*, Le Bon Dieu sans confession*, Le Blé en herbe*, Le Rouge et le noir*, French Cancan, Cela s'appelle l'aurore, Marguerite de la nuit*, La Traversée de Paris*, En cas de malheur*, Le Joueur*, Les Régates de San Francisco*, La Jument verte*, Le Bois des amants*, Tu ne tueras point*, Vive Henri IV, vive l'amour*; Le Comte de Monte Cristo*, Le Meurtrier*, Topkapi* (Dassin, U.S.A., 64), Journal d'une femme en blanc*, Le Franciscain de Bourges*, Les Patates*, Boulevard du rhum.*

161 DRACH, Michel (1930 –). B: Paris. Director. At first assistant to Melville. Also TV work. Ambitious and often compelling productions.

Films (also co-scripted *): *On n'enterre pas le dimanche*, Amélie ou le temps d'aimer*, La bonne occase, Safari diamants*, Elise ou la vraie vie.*

162 DUBOIS, Marie (1937 –). B: Paris. Stage and screen actress. Sincerity and warmth, allied to an almost luminous beauty, have made her a favourite among *Nouvelle Vague* directors.

Main films: *Le Signe du lion, Tirez sur le pianiste, Une Femme est une femme, Jules et Jim, Le Monocle noir, Week-end à Zuydcoote, Le dix-septième ciel, Le Voleur, La grande Vadrouille, Les grandes gueules, La Maison des Bories, BOF Anatomie d'un livreur.*

163 DUBOST, Paulette (1911 –). B: Paris. Stage and screen actress, a specialist in ironic lady's maids.

Main films: *Hôtel du Nord, La Règle du jeu, Le Plaisir, La Fête à Henriette, Lola Montès, Le Déjeuner sur l'herbe, Germinal, Viva Maria.*

164 DULAC, Germaine (1882 – 1942). B: Amiens. D: Paris. Woman director, and a key figure in the *avant-garde*, impressionist and

Mohamed Chouikh and Marie-José Nat in Michel Drach's ELISE OU LA VRAIE VIE

Emmanuelle Riva and Eiji Okada in Resnais's HIROSHIMA MON AMOUR, scripted by Marguerite Duras

surrealist movements of the Twenties. At first drama critic and authoress. 1930 – 40: directed Pathé newsreels. She put her theories about "pure cinema" (visual abstraction) into practice in her shorts *Arabesque* (29), *Thème et variations* (29).

Main features: *Ames de fous, La Cigarette, La Fête espagnole, La souriante Madame Beudet, La Coquille et le clergyman* (script by Antonin ARTAUD).

165 D U L L I N, Charles (1885 – 1949). B: Yennes. D: Paris. Stage producer and actor, held in great respect. His comparatively few film roles all left a deep impression. Many leading actors began their career under his care.

Main films (as actor): *Le Miracle des loups,*

Le Joueur, Les Misérables, Maldone, L'Affaire du courrier de Lyon, Volpone, Quai des Orfèvres, Les Jeux sont faits.

166 D U R A N D, Jean (1882 – 1946). B. and D: Paris. Actor and director, an important pioneer of film comedy. 1900 – 02: worked at the "Chat-Noir" and other Montmartre cabarets. His main themes—the chase, and the smash-up—bordered on the *fantastique*. He made a series of shorts between 1910 and 1922, notably the *Calino, Zigoto,* and *Onésime* series.

167 D U R A S, Marguerite (1914 –   ). B: Giadinh, Indochina. RN: Marguerite Donnadieu. A leading writer of the *Nouveau Roman* school. Scripted several "new cinema" films, including *Barrage contre le Pacifique, Hiroshima mon amour, Moderato Cantabile* (Brook,

France, 60), and *Une aussi longue absence*. She has written and directed two features, both experiments with language, visual and spoken.

Films: *La Musica* (co. dir. Paul Seban), *Détruire dit-elle*.

168 DUVIVIER, Julien (1896 – 1967). B: Lille. Leading director who shot over a hundred films. At first actor. Assistant to L'Herbier and Feuillade (qq.v.). 1940 – 44: U.S.A., where he made *Lydia, Tales of Manhattan, The Imposter*. A fine representative of the naturalist and poetic realist schools. The most creative phase of Duvivier's career was undoubtedly the Thirties. Scripted most of his own films.

Main films: *L'Homme à l'Hispano, David Golder, Poil de Carotte, La Tête d'un homme, Maria Chapdelaine, La Bandera, La belle équipe, Pépé le Moko, Un Carnet de bal, La Fin du jour, La Charrette fantôme, Untel père et fils, Panique, Sous le ciel de Paris, La Fête à Henriette, L'Affaire Maurizius, Marianne de ma jeunesse, Le Temps des assassins, Pot-Bouille, La Femme et le pantin, Marie-Octobre, Le Diable et les dix commandements, Diaboliquement vôtre*.

169 EAUBONNE, Jean D' (1903 –   ). B: Talence. Well-known set designer, at first assistant to Lazare Meerson (q.v.). His restrained and meticulous *décors* left their mark on a whole era of French cinema.

Main films: *Le Sang d'un poète, Pour un sou d'amour, Les Gens du voyage, La Loi du nord, Macadam, Orphée, La Ronde, Le Plaisir, Casque d'Or, La Fête à Henriette, Rue de l'Estrapade, Madame de . . ., Touchez pas au grisbi, Lola Montès, Bitter Victory* (Ray, U.S.A., 57), *Montparnasse 19, Charade* (Donen, U.S.A., 64), *Une Veuve en or, La Route de Salina, Le Cri du cormoran le soir au-dessus des jonques; Laisse aller, c'est une valse*.

170 ENRICO, Robert (1931 –   ). B: Liévin. Director. At first studied at IDHEC. His shorts include the Academy Award-winning *Incident at Owl Creek/La Rivière du hibou* (based on the story by Ambrose Bierce), which was one of three episodes in his feature *Au Cœur de la vie*. A distinctly personal and appealing talent. Also TV work.

Films (also scripted): *Au Cœur de la vie, La belle vie, Les grandes gueules, Les Aventuriers, Tante Zita, Ho!; Un peu, beaucoup passionnément, Boulevard du rhum*.

171 EPSTEIN, Jean (1897 – 1953). B: Warsaw. D: Paris. Director and theorist, a dominant figure of the impressionist *avant-garde* (q.v.) during the Twenties. Wrote several books asserting his belief in the cinema's powers of expression: "Bonjour cinéma" (21), "Le Cinématographe vu de l'Etna" (26), "L'Intelligence d'une machine" (46), "Le Cinéma du diable" (47), and "Esprit de cinéma" (53). In all his films Epstein tried to stress the *photogenic* quality of people and things. His sister, Marie Epstein, often collaborated with him.

Main films: *Cœur fidèle, La belle Nivernaise, Le Lion des Mogols, La Chute de la maison Usher, Finis terrae, Morvran, L'Or des mers, Le Tempestaire* (short, 47).

Pierre Etaix in YOYO

172 ÉTAIX, Pierre (1928–). B: Roanne. Director. At first appeared in cabaret and music hall. Then worked as a gagman for Jacques Tati (q.v.). Made four shorts that focused attention on his clown-like gifts: *Rupture* (61), *Heureux anniversaire, Nous n'irons plus au bois* (64), and *Insomnie* (65). His features have shown him to be a major comedy director. Acted in *Pickpocket*.

Films (all scripted in collab. with J-C. Carrière, q.v.): *Le Soupirant, Yoyo, Tant qu'on a la santé, Le grand amour, Pays de Cocagne.*

173 EUSTACHE, Jean (1938–). Director. At first assistant and editor. A gifted young film-maker whose work is made up of both documentary and fictional elements. Acted: *Week-end.*

Films: *Les mauvaises fréquentations, Le Père Noël a les yeux bleus, La Rosière de Pessac, Le Cochon* (co-dir. Jean-Michel Barjol) (last two for TV).

174 EVEIN, Bernard (1929–). B: Saint Nazaire. Designer for theatre and cinema, who came to the fore (at first in collaboration with Jacques Saulnier, q.v.) thanks to working on several *Nouvelle Vague* productions.

Main films (some with Saulnier*): *Les Amants*, Les Cousins*, Les Jeux de l'amour*, A double tour*, Les 400 Coups, L'Année dernière à Marienbad, Une Femme est une femme, Lola, Zazie dans le métro, Cléo de 5 à 7, Le Combat dans l'île, Vie privée, Le Jour et l'heure, Le Feu follet, Les Parapluies de Cherbourg, L'Insoumis, Viva Maria, Les Demoiselles de Rochefort.*

175 FALCONETTI (1901 – 1946). B: Paris. D: Buenos Aires. Actress, famous for just one film—Dreyer's *La Passion de Jeanne d'Arc*. By immersing herself completely in the role, and agreeing to the great man's stern supervision, she brought Joan overwhelmingly to life. Her grandson, Gérard Falconetti (*b* 1949) has just started a career as an actor—in *Le Genou de Claire*.

176 FERNANDEL (1903–1971). B: Marseille. RN: Ferdinand Joseph Désiré Contandin. Actor. Began in operetta, café concerts and music hall. He has starred in over a hundred films, establishing himself as a comedian of the top rank.

Main films: *Les Gaîtés de l'escadron, Le Rosier de Madame Husson, Angèle, François Ier, Un Carnet de bal, Regain, Le Schpountz, Fric-frac, La Fille du puisatier, Naïs, Topaze* (51), *L'Auberge rouge, Ali Baba, La Vache et le prisonnier, Around the World in 80 Days* (M. Anderson, U.S.A., 56), *Le Diable et les dix commandements, La Cuisine au beurre, La Bourse et la vie, Le Voyage du père, Heureux qui comme Ulysse,* as well as three *Don Camillo* films (in Italy).

177 FERRY, Jean (1906 –   ). B: Capens. Noted scriptwriter.

Main films: *Quai des Orfèvres, Manon, Miquette et sa mère, Cela s'appelle l'aurore, Babette s'en va-t-en guerre, Vie privée, Pas question le samedi.*

Falconetti in LA PASSION DE JEANNE D'ARC

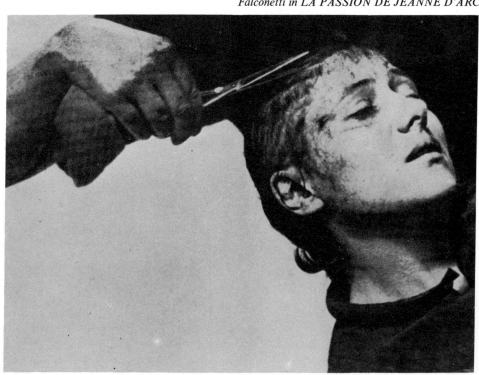

Above: Edwige Feuillère. At right: Feuillade's
LES VAMPIRES

178   FESCOURT, Henri (1880 – 1966). B:
Béziers. D: Neuilly. An important director of
the Twenties, whose many films were typical of
the realistic tendency of the French cinema at
that period. 1931: Sweden, where he shot
Serments and *Service de nuit*. Fescourt wrote
several books, including "Le Cinéma des
origines à nos jours" (a kind of collective
encyclopaedia, 32), and "La Foi et les mon-
tagnes" (61), an interesting set of memoirs.
    Main films: *Mathias Sandorf, Rouletabille,*
Mandrin, Les Misérables, Monte Cristo.

179   FEUILLADE, Louis (1874 – 1925). B:
Lunel. D: Nice. Major director, regarded as the
pioneer of the crime "serial," which he ap-
proached in a naturalistic vein. At first
journalist, then scriptwriter for Pathé. From
1906 onwards he directed a large number of
minor films at Gaumont. He made his name
with his serials: *Fantômas, Les Vampires,*
Judex, La nouvelle mission de Judex, Tih-Minh,
Barrabas, Les deux gamines, L'Orpheline,
Parisette, Le Fils du flibustier.

180   FEUILLÈRE, Edwige (1907 –   ).
B: Vesoul. RN: Edwige Caroline Cunati.
Stage and screen actress. Her distinguished
playing has fitted her naturally for several roles
as the *grande dame* in French cinema.
    Main films: *Lucrèce Borgia, Sans lendemain,*
De Mayerling à Sarajevo, La Duchesse de
Langeais, L'Aigle à deux têtes, Le Blé en herbe,
En cas de malheur, La Princesse de Clèves,
Clair de terre.

181   FEYDER, Jacques (1888 – 1948). B:
Ixelles (Brussels). D: Geneva. RN: Jacques
Frédérix. A major director of the Thirties and a
leading representative of the realist school. At

59

first actor, then assistant. Began directing in 1915 with some fifteen short comedies.

Films: *L'Atlantide, Crainquebille, Visages d'enfants, L'Image, Gribiche, Carmen, Au pays du roi lépreux, Thérèse Raquin* (28), *Les nouveaux messieurs*. In U.S.A. (1929–31): six films, French (or German) versions of American productions except *The Kiss*. In France: *Le grand jeu, Pension Mimosas, La Kermesse héroïque*. In Britain: *Knight without Armour*. In France: *Les Gens du voyage, La loi du nord, Une Femme disparaît, Macadam* (completed by Marcel Blistène, 46).

182 FRANJU, Georges (1912–   ). B: Fougères. Director. Since 1930: journalist. Co-founder of the Cinémathèque française (q.v.) with Henri Langlois (also q.v.) in 1936. An outstanding short film specialist during the Fifties. Also stage designer. Franju's particular gift lies in perceiving the sinister, sometimes fiendish aspects of everyday reality (the abattoirs of *Le Sang des bêtes*, the asylum of *La Tête contre les murs*).

Films (shorts): *Le Métro* (34), *Le Sang des bêtes* (49), *En passant par la Lorraine* (50), *Hôtel des Invalides* (51), *Le grand Méliès* (52), *M. et Mme Curie* (53), *Les Poussières* (54), *Navigation marchande* (54), *A propos d'une rivière* (55), *Mon Chien* (55), *Le Théâtre National Populaire* (56), *Sur le pont d'Avignon* (56), *Notre-Dame, cathédrale de Paris* (57), *La première nuit* (58). Features: *La Tête contre les murs, Les Yeux sans visage, Pleins feux sur l'assassin, Thérèse Desqueyroux, Judex, Thomas l'Imposteur, La Faute de l'Abbé Mouret*.

183 FRESNAY, Pierre (1897–   ). B: Paris. Well-established stage (Comédie française 1915–27) and screen actor, often found in aristocratic roles. 1915: enters cinema.

Main films: *Marius, Fanny, César, La grande illusion, Le Puritain, La Charrette fantôme, L'Assassin habite au 21, Le Corbeau, Le*

Feyder's LA KERMESSE HÉROÏQUE

Voyageur sans bagage, Monsieur Vincent, Dieu a besoin des hommes, Le Défroqué, Les Aristocrates, L'Homme aux clés d'or, Les Vieux de la vieille.

184 FRESSON, Bernard (1931–). Stage and screen actor. His eagerness and friendly disposition have enlivened his various supporting roles.

Main films: *Hiroshima mon amour, Le Testament du Dr. Cordelier, La Bride sur le cou, La Guerre est finie, Jeudi on chantera comme Dimanche* (de Heusch, Belgium, 67), *Loin du Vietnam, Je t'aime, je t'aime, Tante Zita, Adieu l'ami, La Prisonnière, Z, L'Américain, Le Portrait de Marianne, Un Condé, Max et les ferrailleurs.*

185 FREY, Samy (1937–). B: Paris. Stage and screen actor. Dark, intriguing personality whose career has been so far somewhat limited.

Main films: *La Vérité, Cléo de 5 à 7, Thérèse Desqueyroux, Bande à part, Qui êtes-vous Polly Maggoo?*

186 FUNÈS, Louis de (1914–). B: Courbevoie. Stage and screen actor (at first in cabaret) who has become the top comedy draw at the French box-office thanks to his zany humour.

Main films: *Antoine et Antoinette, Les sept péchés capitaux, Le Blé en herbe, Napoléon* (54); *Papa, Maman, la bonne et moi; La Traversée de Paris, Candide, La belle Américaine, Le Gendarme de Saint-Tropez, Fantômas, Le Corniaud, Oscar* (also co-scripted), *Le petit baigneur, La grande vadrouille, Le Tatoué, Hibernatus, Sur un arbre perché.*

187 GABIN, Jean (1904–). B: Mériel. RN: Jean-Alexis Moncorgé. One of the most famous of all French actors. At first worked in music hall, operetta, and theatre. Since the Fifties Gabin has been generally considered the top box-office star in France. 1941–45: U.S.A.

Main films: *Les Gaîtés de l'escadron, Maria Chapdelaine, La Bandera, Variétés, La belle*

équipe, *Les Bas-fonds, Pépé le Moko, La grande illusion, Gueule d'amour, Quai des brumes, La bête humaine, Le Jour se lève, Remorques, Au-delà des grilles, La Marie du port, Le Plaisir, La Vérité sur Bébé Donge, La Minute de Vérité, Touchez pas au grisbi, L'Air de Paris, Le Port du désir, French Cancan, Napoléon* (54), *Razzia sur la chnouf, La Traversée de Paris, Le Cas du Dr. Laurent, Crime et châtiment, Maigret tend un piège, Les Misérables, En cas de malheur, Les grandes familles, Le Baron de l'Ecluse, Le Président, Le Vieux de la vieille, Un Singe en hiver, Mélodie en sous-sol, Monsieur, Le Tonnerre de dieu, Le Tatoué, Le Clan des Siciliens, Le Chat.*

188 GAINSBOURG, Serge (1928 –). B: Paris. Composer (also song writer) whose work has been enormously popular in recent years.

Main films (as composer): *L'Eau à la bouche, L'Espion, L'Horizon, Si j'étais un espion, L'Une et l'autre, Manon 70*, and *. Also acted (to striking effect): *Mister Freedom, Vivre la nuit, Paris n'existe pas*, Les Chemins de Katmandou*, Erotissimo, Cannabis*.*

189 GANCE, Abel (1889 –). B: Paris. Very important director, notably in the Twenties, when, on the fringes of the *avant-garde* he made several major contributions to film technique (Polyvision, editing methods, etc.). At first stage actor and playwright. 1909 – 12: scripts for Gaumont and Film d'Art. 1911 – 1917: some twenty shorts, including *La Folie du Dr Tube* and *La Zone de la mort.*

Films: *Mater dolorosa, La dixième symphonie, J'accuse!, La Roue, Au secours, Napoléon* (27), *La Fin du monde, Mater dolorosa* (sound version), *Le Maître de forges, Poliche, La Dame aux camélias, Napoléon Bonaparte* (sound version), *Le Roman d'un jeune homme pauvre,*

Lucrèce Borgia, Un grand amour de Beethoven, Jérôme Perreau, Le Voleur de femmes, J'accuse! (sound version), *Louise, Paradis perdu, La Vénus aveugle, Le Capitaine Fracasse, La Tour de Nesle, Austerlitz, Cyrano et d'Artagnan.* Gance has also published a group of imaginative essays about the cinema, entitled "Prismes" (30).

190 GARREL, Philippe (1948 –). Director, noted for the youthful aggression and intensity of his films. At first made two good shorts: *Droit de visite* (66), *Les Enfants désaccordés* (67).

Films: *Anémone, Marie pour mémoire, Le Révélateur, La Concentration, Le Lit de la Vierge, La Cicatrice intérieure.*

191 GATTI, Armand (1924 –). B: Monaco. Director. Also journalist, poet, dramatic adviser, and scriptwriter for Chris Marker (*Dimanche à Pékin, Lettre de Sibérie*),

Opposite: Jean Gabin

and J.-C. Bonnardot (*Morambong*). An original and engaging director.

Films (also scripted): *L'Enclos, L'autre Cristobal* (in Cuba).

192 GAUMONT, Léon (1863 – 1946). B: Paris. D: Sainte-Maxime. An important producer. At first a businessman and then a manufacturer of film equipment, he founded his own production company in 1903. This firm, Gaumont (like Pathé) is still one of the most powerful French film organisations. Directors such as Emile Cohl, Jean Durand, Louis Feuillade, Henri Fescourt, Marcel L'Herbier, Jacques Feyder, and René Clair (qq.v.) began their career in his studios. Later in life he became interested in colour and sound, and until his retirement in 1929 he supervised all the company's productions with dynamic verve.

193 GAVRAS, Costa (1933 –). B: Athens. Director. 1949: to France. At first assistant to Clément, Clair, Giono, Demy. Costa Gavras has made a considerable impact both on French and foreign filmgoers with his hard-hitting thrillers, often with political overtones.

Films (also co-scripted): *Compartiment tueurs, Un Homme de trop, Z, L'Aveu.*

194 GÉGAUFF, Paul (1922 –). B: Blotsheim (Haut-Rhin). Scriptwriter for several key *Nouvelle Vague* productions, particularly those of Chabrol* (q.v.). At first novelist. Acted in *Week-end*. As director: *Le Reflux.*

Main films: *Les Cousins*, A double tour*, Les bonnes femmes*, Plein soleil, Les Godelureaux*, Les plus belles escroqueries du monde* (* episode), *Les grands chemins, Le Scandale*, Les Biches*, More, Que la bête meure*, Les Novices.*

195 GÉLIN, Daniel (1921 –). B: Angers. Stage and screen actor. His distinguished presence has brought him success in the cinema, although in *Edouard et Caroline* he proved himself an excellent light comedian.

Main films: *Premier rendez-vous, Martin Roumagnac, Rendez-vous de Juillet, La Ronde, Edouard et Caroline, Les Mains sales, Le Plaisir, La Minute de vérité, Rue de l'Estrapade, Sang et lumière, L'Affaire Maurizius, Napoléon* (54), *Mort en fraude, Le Testament d'Orphée, Austerlitz, La Morte-saison des amours, La Proie pour l'ombre, Vacances portugaises, Climats, La bonne soupe, La Ligne de démarcation, La Trêve, Détruire dit-elle, Le Souffle au cœur.* As director and actor: *Les Dents longues.*

196 GILLES, Guy (1940 –). B: Algiers. Director. At first assistant and short film specialist—*Soleil éteint* (59), *Au Biseau des baisers* (60), *Mohamed dit Alain* (60), *Melancholia* (61) etc. Acted in *Tire-au-flanc* (61). A mannered, intimate director.

Films: *L'Amour à la mer, Au Pan coupé, Clair de terre, Mille Baisers de Florence.*

197 GIOVANNI, José (1923 –). B: Paris. Director. At first novelist and crime

Buñuel's BELLE DE JOUR. Geneviève Page (left) and Catherine Deneuve in the parlour.

Jacques Demy's LES PARAPLUIES DE CHER-
BOURG. Nino Castelnuovo and Catherine Deneuve
in the final sequence of this French musical. Photo:
Parc Film.

Annie Girardot and Jean-Paul Belmondo in UN HOMME QUI ME PLAÎT

thriller specialist. Scriptwriter for Becker, Sautet, Deray, and Melville (qq.v.); has adapted and directed some of his own novels for the screen. His script work includes *Rififi à Tokyo, Symphonie pour un massacre, Le Trou, Classe tous risques, Le deuxième souffle* (dialogue only), *Le Clan des Siciliens*.

Films as director: *La Loi du survivant, Le Rapace, Dernier domicile connu, Un aller simple*.

198 GIRARDOT, Annie (1931 –   ). B: Paris. Actress, whose vitality and sensual appeal have taken her to stardom during the past ten years. Trained at the Conservatoire. Also stage, TV, radio, and cabaret work.

Main films: *L'Homme aux clés d'or, Le Rouge est mis, Maigret tend un piège, Recours en grâce, La Proie pour l'ombre, Rocco e i suoi fratelli* (Visconti, Italy, 60), *Smog* (Rossi, Italy, 61), *Le Vice et la vertu, I compagni* (Monicelli, Italy, 63), *La bonne soupe, La donna scimmia* (Ferreri, Italy, 64), *Un Monsieur de compagnie, Trois chambres à Manhattan, L'Or du duc(?), Vivre pour vivre, Les Gauloises bleues, It Rains in My Village* (Petrović, Yugoslavia, 68), *Dillinger e' morto* (Ferreri, Italy, 69), *Erotissimo, Metti una sera a cena* (Patroni Griffi, Italy, 69), *Il seme dell' uomo* (Ferreri, Italy, 69), *Un Homme qui me plait, Les Novices, Mourir d'aimer*.

199 GIVRAY, Claude de (1933 –   ). B: Nice. Director. At first critic, then assistant to

Chabrol, Truffaut and others. He has been a regular scriptwriter for Truffaut's films.

Films: *Tire-au-flanc, Une grosse tête, Un Mari à prix fixe, L'Amour à la chaîne.*

200 GODARD, Jean-Luc (1930 –   ). B: Paris. The most famous director of the *Nouvelle Vague*—provocative and original both in his subject matter and approach to cinema, and showing a taste for black humour (at least until his most recent phase). At first critic on *Cahiers du Cinéma*. Then shorts: *Opération béton* (54), *Une Femme coquette* (55), *Tous les garçons s'appellent Patrick* (57), *Charlotte et son Jules* (58), *Une Histoire d'eau* (co-dir. Truffaut, 58).

Films (also scripted): *A bout de souffle, Le petit soldat, Une Femme est une femme, Les sept péchés capitaux* (*La Paresse* episode), *Vivre sa vie, Les Carabiniers, Rogopag* (*Il mondo nuovo* episode, Italy, 62), *Le Mépris, Les plus belles escroqueries du monde* (*Le grand escroc* episode, cut from release version), *Bande à part, Une Femme mariée, Alphaville, Pierrot le fou, Paris vu par . . .* (*Montparnasse-Levallois* episode), *Masculin féminin, Made in USA, Le plus vieux métier du monde* (*L'Amour en l'an 2000* episode), *Deux ou trois choses que je sais d'elle, La Chinoise, Week-end, Amore e rabbia* (*L'Amore* episode, Italy, 68), *Loin du Vietnam* (one episode), *Le gai savoir* (for TV), *Un Film comme les autres, One plus one* (in Britain), *British Sounds/See You at Mao* (for TV, co-dir. Jean-Henri Roger, in Britain), *One American Movie/1 a.m.* (in U.S.A.), *Pravda* (in Czechoslovakia), *Le Vent d'Est,*

Jean-Pierre Léaud in Godard's MADE IN USA

Brigitte Bardot and Michel Piccoli in Godard's LE MÉPRIS. At right: Godard

Lotte in Italia (both in Italy), *Jusqu'à la victoire* (in Palestine), *Vladimir et Rosa, Procès à Chicago*.

201 GRÉMILLON, Jean (1902 – 1959). B: Bayeux. D: Paris. Director, Composer. At first shorts, including the superb *Tour au large* (26), which is among the finest examples of the impressionist *avant-garde*. 1933 – 35: Spain. An ambitious and painstaking film-maker who was often prevented by production troubles from fully expressing himself in the cinema. Wrote the music for most of his own films.

Films: *Maldone, Gardiens de phare, La petite Lise, Daïnah la métisse, Pour un sou d'amour, La dolorosa, Centinela alerta, Pattes de mouches, Gueule d'amour, L'étrange M. Victor, Remorques, Lumière d'été, Le Ciel est à*

vous, Le 6 Juin à l'aube, Pattes blanches, L'étrange Madame X, L'Amour d'une femme. Towards the end of his life, Grémillon again turned to shorts, with some remarkable results, including *Les Charmes de l'existence* (co-dir. Pierre Kast, 49), *Les Désastres de la guerre* (51), *Haute Lisse* (56), and *André Masson et les quatre éléments* (58).

202 GRÉVILLE, Edmond T. (1906 – 1966). B: Nice. Director. His commercial films often had style and atmosphere. Also novelist and playwright. 1929 – 30: assistant to Dupont and Gance. Acted in *Sous les toits de Paris.*

Main films: *Le Train des suicidés, Mademoiselle Docteur, Menaces, Le Port du désir, Le Diable souffle, Les Mains d'Orlac, L'Accident.*

203 GRIGNON, Marcel (1914 –). B: Paris. Director of photography, noted for his detailed knowledge of technique. 1933: enters cinema as camera assistant.

Main films: *L'ingénue libertine, Un grand patron, Rue de l'Estrapade, L'Amérique insolite,*

Les Liaisons dangereuses, Un Taxi pour Tobrouk, La Proie pour l'ombre, Le Vice et la vertu, Fantômas, Paris brûle-t-il?, Hibernatus, The Fixer (Frankenheimer, U.S.A., 68).

204 GRIMAULT, Paul (1905 –). B: Neuilly-sur-Seine. Much respected animator. At first made publicity cartoons (1936 – 39), then turned to more original fiction animation.

Main films (shorts): *Les Passagers de la Grande Ourse* (39), *Le Marchand de notes* (42), *L'Epouvantail* (43), *Le Voleur de paratonnerres* (46), *La Flûte magique* (46), *Le petit soldat* (47). Feature: *La Bergère et le ramoneur.* Grimault was persuaded to re-enter the advertising film world as a producer. He has also coached several talented young animators (Laguionie, Collombat). Returned to directing with a short, *Le Diamant* (70).

205 GRUEL, Henri (1923 –). B: Paris. Writer and director of animated cartoons. His freshness and wit have helped to revitalise the genre.

Main films (shorts): *Martin et Gaston* (53), *Gitanos et papillons* (54), *Le Voyage de Badabou* (55), *La Joconde* (58), *Monsieur Tête* (co. Jan Lenica, 59), *Notre-Dame de Paris* (61). One feature (fictional): *Le Roi du village.* Now working once more in advertising films.

206 GUITRY, Sacha (1895 - 1957). B: St. Petersburg. D: Paris. Actor, dramatist, director, and a prominent figure in the Paris entertainment world between the wars. He adapted most of his plays successfully for the cinema, usually appearing in them himself to such a narcissistic degree as to offset some of his legendary wit and attractive personality.

Opposite: Sacha Guitry and Jacqueline Delubac in the former's LE ROMAN D'UN TRICHEUR

Main films (as director and scriptwriter, some also acted*): *Le Roman d'un tricheur*, *Faisons un rêve*, *Les Perles de la couronne** (co-dir. Christian-Jaque), *Le Mot de Cambronne*, *Remontons les Champs-Elysées**, *Ils étaient neuf célibataires**, *Le Diable boiteux*, *La Poison*, *La Vie d'un honnête homme*, *Si Versailles m'était conté**, *Napoléon** (54), *Si Paris nous était conté**.

207 HAMMAN, Joe (1895 –). B: Paris. Actor. The first "cowboy" in French cinema, appearing in several films around 1910, mostly directed by him. Featured in the *Arizona Bill* and *Nick Carter* series. From 1921: producer of numerous adventure films. From 1945: executive producer and technical adviser. Hamman has written two vivid memoirs: "Sur les pistes du Far West" (61), and "Du Far West à Montmartre" (62).

208 HANOUN, Marcel (1929 –). B: Tunis. Director. At first journalist, then specialist in short films, including *Gérard de la nuit* (55). His features are studies of moral problems, shot and edited in a very unusual style.
Films: *Une simple histoire*, *Le huitième jour*, *Octobre à Madrid*, *L'authentique procès de Carl-Emmanuel Jung*, *L'Eté*, *L'Hiver*, *Le Printemps*.

209 HAYER, Nicolas (1898 –). B: Paris. Director of photography. 1924: photographer in Indochina. 1928 – 34: international work for M-G-M. Famous for catching the realism as well as the exotic feel of a location.
Main films: *Dernier atout*, *Le Corbeau*, *Falbalas*, *Panique*, *La Chartreuse de Parme*, *Un Homme marche dans la ville*, *Orphée*, *Sous le ciel de Paris*, *Deux hommes dans Manhattan*, *Le Signe du Lion*, *Leviathan*, *Le Doulos*.

210 HERMAN, Jean (1933 –). B: Pagny-sur-Moselle. Director. 1955: film

school. At first shorts, including *Actua-Tilt* (60). An interesting director who has worked in several *genres* and has made numerous TV films.
Films: *Le Chemin de la mauvaise route*, *Le Dimanche de la vie*, *Adieu l'ami*, *Popsy Pop*.

211 HONEGGER, Arthur (1892 – 1955). B: Le Havre. D: Geneva. Composer. Arranged the music for Abel Gance's *La Roue* and later developed this into a symphonic poem entitled *Pacific 231*.
Main film scores: *Napoléon* (27), *Les Misérables*, *Crime et châtiment*, *Mayerling*, *Un Revenant*. His oratorio *Jeanne au bûcher* inspired Rossellini's film *Giovanna d'Arco al rogo*.

212 HOSSEIN, Robert (1927 –). B: Paris. Actor and director. His powerful physical presence has made Hossein an ideal and often

tragic "heavy." His own films are usually violent and dramatic.

Main films (as actor): *Du Rififi chez les hommes, Sait-on jamais, La Sentence, Le Repos du guerrier, Le Vice et la vertu, Les grands chemins, Le Meurtrier, Lamiel, La Musica, La Leçon particulière,* and the *Angélique* films. As director (also co-scripted and acted): *Les Salauds vont en enfer, Pardonnez nos offenses, Toi le venin, La Nuit des espions, Les Scélérats, Le Goût de la violence, Le Jeu de la vérité, Mort d'un tueur, Le Vampire de Düsseldorf, Les Yeux cernés, J'ai tué Raspoutine; Une Corde, un colt; Point de chute.*

213 HUBERT, Roger (1903–). B: Montreuil-sur-Bois. Director of photography, held in high esteem for his work during the Thirties and Forties.

Main films: *Napoléon* (co., 27), *Mater dolorosa, La Chienne* (co.), *Pension Mimosas, Jenny, Volpone, La Loi du nord, Les Visiteurs du soir, L'éternel retour, Les Enfants du paradis, Les Amants de Bras-Mort, La Fête à Henriette, L'Air de Paris.*

214 HUNEBELLE, André (1896–). B: Meudon. Director. Prolific run of box-office successes, generally lacking in artistic quality.

Main films: *Millionaire d'un jour, Méfiez-vous des blondes, Ma Femme est formidable, Mon Mari est merveilleux, Casino de Paris, Les trois Mousquetaires, Les Mystères de Paris, Fantômas.*

215 ICHAC, Marcel (1906–). B: Rueil. Director. Specialist in mountaineering documentaries and films about exploration.

Films (main shorts): *Karakoram* (36), *Pélerins de La Mecque* (40), *A l'assaut des Aiguilles du Diable* (42), *Ski de France* (47). Features: *Victoire sur l'Anapurna, Les Etoiles de Midi.*

216 I.D.H.E.C. "Institut des Hautes Etudes Cinématographiques." A film school, established in 1943 at Nice; transferred to Paris in 1944 after the Liberation. Its real value hardly lives up to its international reputation. Students from all over the world attend IDHEC, but few *cinéastes* of real talent have developed there.

217 IMPRESSIONISM. A film movement of the Twenties, so called by Louis Delluc (q.v.) because of its plastic relationship to the experiments (from 1865 onwards) by such painters as Cézanne, Manet, Monet, Pissarro, Renoir, and Seurat, experiments that tried to present a subjective vision of reality by means of light. The term was doubtless applied to the cinema in reaction to German expressionism.

Among the most typical impressionist films were *La Fête espagnole* and *Fièvre* (Delluc), *La souriante Madame Beudet* (Dulac), *Eldorado* (L'Herbier), *La Chute de la Maison Usher* and *Cœur fidèle* (Epstein), *En rade* (Cavalcanti), *Ménilmontant* (Kirsanoff), *La petite marchande d'allumettes* (Renoir), *Tour au large* (Grémillon), and *Nogent, Eldorado du dimanche* (Carné).

Impressionism made use of technical effects such as superimposition, soft focus, distortion, rapid camera movements etc., so as to give the spectator a subjective, interior impression of life.

218 ISOU, Jean-Isidore (1925–). B: Botosani (Romania). Writer, and founder of the *lettriste* movement which tried to revolutionise literature, painting, and cinema. In his feature film, *Traité de bave et d'éternité,* Isou illustrated his desire to "destroy the image."

219 IVENS, Joris (1898–). B: Nijmegen. Dutch director, specialising in social and political documentaries. Since 1958 he has made France his base and some of his films have been either directed or produced there.

Films (in France): *La Seine a rencontré Paris* (58), *Le Mistral* (64), *Le Ciel, la terre* (65), *Dix-septième parallèle* (67), *Loin du Vietnam* (one episode), *Le Peuple et ses fusils* (69).

220 J A R R E, Maurice (1924 –   ). B: Lyon. Composer. Wrote some sensitive and fastidious scores for *Nouvelle Vague* films before veering towards big international productions and repetitive tunes. 1950: in charge of music at the TNP.

Main films: *Hôtel des Invalides* (Franju), *Toute la mémoire du monde* (Resnais), *Le bel indifférent* (Demy), *La Tête contre les murs, Les Dragueurs, Les Yeux sans visage, Thérèse Desqueyroux, The Longest Day* (Zanuck, U.S.A., 61), *Recours en grâce, Pleins feux sur*

l'assassin, Les Dimanches de Ville-d'Avray, Lawrence of Arabia (Lean, Britain, 62), *Mourir à Madrid, Les Animaux, Behold a Pale Horse* (Zinnemann, U.S.A., 64), *The Train* (Frankenheimer, U.S.A., 64), *Week-end à Zuydcoote, Doctor Zhivago* (Lean, Britain, 65), *The Collector* (Wyler, Britain, 65), *Paris brûle-t-il?, Grand Prix* (Frankenheimer, U.S.A., 66), *The Professionals* (Brooks, U.S.A., 66), *Night of the Generals* (Litvak, Britain/France, 66), *Barbarella, The Fixer* (Frankenheimer, U.S.A., 68), *Isadora* (Reisz, Britain, 69), *The Damned* (Visconti, 69), *Ryan's Daughter* (Lean, Britain, 70).

221 J A U B E R T, Maurice (1900 – 1940). B: Nice, D. Azerailles. The best French film composer of the Thirties, admired for the

Claudine Auger with Michel Duchaussoy in JEU DE MASSACRE

beauty and originality of his themes, especially the atmospheric scores he wrote for Marcel Carné*.

Main films: *Le petit Chaperon Rouge, Quatorze Juillet, L'Affaire est dans le sac, Le dernier milliardaire, Zéro de conduite, L'Atalante, Un Carnet de bal, La Fin du jour, Drôle de drame*, Hôtel du Nord*, Quai des brumes*, Le Jour se lève*.*

222 JEANSON, Henri (1900 – 1970). B: Paris. Scriptwriter, most famous (especially in the Thirties) for his biting wit and his flair for punch lines. At first journalist, film critic and dramatist.

Main films: *Pépé le Moko, Un Carnet de bal, Entrée des artistes, Hôtel du Nord, La Nuit fantastique, Boule de suif, Les Maudits, Fanfan la Tulipe, La Fête à Henriette, La Vache et le prisonnier, Le Glaive et la balance.* As director (and scriptwriter): *Lady Paname.*

223 JESSUA, Alain (1932 –   ). B: Paris. Director. Assistant to Becker, Ophuls, Y. Allégret, and Carné (qq.v.). Began his career with a short, *Léon la Lune* (Prix Jean Vigo, 57). Jessua is fascinated by the psychological side of things, and his features contain deep and troubled thoughts beneath their surface wit.

Films (also scripted): *La Vie à l'envers, Jeu de massacre, Les Panthères blanches.*

224 JOANNON, Léo (1904 –1969). B: Aix-en-Provence. Prolific director whose productions have a purely commercial importance.

Main films: *Alerte en Méditerranée, Le Carrefour des enfants perdus, Le Défroqué, L'Homme aux clés d'or, Tant d'amour perdu, Fort du fou.*

225 JOBERT, Marlène (1940–   ). B: Algiers. Stage and screen actress. Launched by Godard (q.v.), she owes her dynamic success to her youthful charm and lightheartedness.

Main films: *Masculin féminin, Alexandre le bienheureux, Le Voleur, Faut pas prendre les enfants du bon dieu pour des canards sauvages, L'Astragale, Le Passager de la pluie, Dernier domicile connu, Les Mariés de l'An Deux, La Poudre d'escampette.*

226 JOUVET, Louis (1887 – 1951). B: Crozon. D: Paris. An almost legendary stage and screen actor. Several major parts were created by Jouvet's strength of personality, his sly, quizzical wit, and distinctive presence. 1907: enters theatre. 1912 – 1917: works with Jacques Copeau at the "Vieux Colombier." 1939 – 45: in Switzerland and South America.

Main films: *Topaze, Knock, La Kermesse héroïque, Les Bas-fonds, Mademoiselle Docteur, Un Carnet de bal, Drôle de drame, L'Alibi, La Marseillaise, Entrée des artistes, Hôtel du Nord, La Fin du jour, Volpone, Untel père et fils, Un Revenant, Quai des Orfèvres.*

Above: Nelly Kaplan. Opposite: Anna Karina and Micheline Presle in LA RELIGIEUSE

227 KAPLAN, Nelly (1934 –   ). Woman director, born in Argentina. At first journalist, writer, and assistant to Gance (q.v.). Made some fine short films on painting and related topics: *Gustave Moreau* (61), *Rodolphe Bresdin* (62), *Les Années 25, Abel Gance hier et demain, A la source la femme aimée* (65), *Le Regard Picasso* (67).

Films: *La Fiancée du pirate, Le Collier de Ptyx.*

Une Femme est une femme, Cléo de 5 à 7, Vivre sa vie, Dragées au poivre, Les quatre vérités, Bande à part, Le Voleur du Tibidabo, La Ronde (64), *Alphaville, Pierrot le fou, La Religieuse, Made in USA, L'Etranger* (Visconti, Italy/France/Algeria, 67), *Lamiel, The Magus* (Guy Green, Britain, 68), *Justine* (Cukor, U.S.A., 68), *Michael Kohlhaas* (Schlöndorff, West Germany, 69), *Laughter in the Dark* (Richardson, Britain, 69), *L'Alliance, Rendez-vous à Braye* (A. Delvaux, 71).

228 KARINA, Anna (1940 –   ). B: Copenhagen. RN: Hanne Karin Blarke Bayer. Actress. At first model. Discovered and launched by Godard (q.v.), she rapidly became (with her somewhat exotic appeal) the key star of the *Nouvelle Vague.*

Main films: *Le petit soldat, Ce Soir ou jamais,*

229 KARMITZ, Marin (1940 –   ). Director. At first shorts: *Les Idoles* (63), *Nuit noire Calcutta* (scripted by Marguerite DURAS, 64), *Comédie* (based on Beckett's play, 66). A likable and promising young director.

Films: *Sept jours ailleurs, Camarades.*

230 KAST, Pierre (1920 –). B: Paris. Director. At first critic on *Cahiers du Cinéma*, then also *Positif*. 1948 – 49: assistant to Jean Grémillon (q.v.). Has also worked with Renoir, Clément, and Preston Sturges. Several outstanding shorts, including *Les Charmes de l'Existence* (co-dir. Grémillon, 49), *Les Désastres de la guerre* (51), *Ledoux architecte maudit* (53), *La Brûlure de mille soleils* (science fiction, 65). All Kast's carefully-made films reveal his intelligent, analytical approach to life.

Films (also scripted*): *Un Amour de poche, Merci Natercia, Le bel âge*, La Morte-saison des amours, Vacances portugaises, Le Grain de sable, Drôle de jeu*, Macumba**. Television series: *La Chute de l'Empire romain* (67), *Carnets brésiliens* (68).

231 KAUFMAN, Boris. B: Bialystock. Well-known director of photography. Born in Poland; brother of Dziga Vertov and Mikhaïl Kaufman. Emigrated to France with his parents while still very young, then to U.S.A. in 1942. During his spell in France, he shot a number of films, notably those of Jean Vigo (q.v.): *A propos de Nice, Taris, Zéro de conduite, L'Atalante*.

232 KELBER, Michel (1908 –). B: Kiev, Ukraine. Director of photography. At first studied art and architecture. 1929: entered films as assistant to Harry Stradling at Gaumont and Paramount studios, Paris. 1933: becomes dir. of phot.

Main films: *Un Carnet de bal* (co.), *Une*

Jeanne Moreau in MATA-HARI AGENT H-21, photographed by Michel Kelber

Femme disparaît, Ruy Blas, Le Diable au corps, Les Parents terribles, La Beauté du diable, Le Rouge et le noir, French Cancan, Les Salauds vont en enfer, Mata Hari agent H-21, Journal d'une femme en blanc, Le Franciscain de Bourges.

233 KIRSANOFF, Dimitri (1899 – 1957). B: Dorpat. D: Paris. Director, born in Russia. His French work belonged to the impressionist and *avant-garde* schools (qq.v.). After 1930 his output was purely commercial, save perhaps for one short, *Deux Amis* (45). Main films: *Ménilmontant, Brumes d'automne.*

234 KLEIN, William (1928 –). B: New York. American photographer living in France since 1948. Has made short and medium-length *cinéma-vérité* films for TV and cinema, including *Broadway by Light* (58), *Le Business et la mode* (61), *Cassius le Grand, La grande Hernie, Le grand homme* (64–65, three films on the boxer Cassius Clay, later combined into a feature-length release entitled *Cassius le Grand*). Acted in *La Jetée.* Artistic adviser on *Zazie dans le métro.*

Other films (also scripted): *Qui êtes-vous, Polly Maggoo?, Loin du Vietnam* (one episode), *Mister Freedom; Eldridge Cleaver, Black Panther* (doc.).

235 KORBER, Serge (1936 –). Director. At first assistant to Baratier. Comedy shorts include *Delphica* (62), *La Dame à la longue vue* (62), *L'Epouse infernale* (63), *Eve sans trêve* (63), *Un Jour à Paris* (64), *La Demoiselle de Saint-Florentin* (65). Korber's shorts and features have an unusually discreet, sometimes lyrical quality. Acted in *Cléo de 5 à 7* and *Tire-au-flanc.*

Films: *Le dix-septième ciel, Un Idiot à Paris, La petite Vertu, L'Homme orchestre, Sur un arbre perché.*

236 KOSMA, Joseph (1905 –1969). B: Budapest. Composer. From 1933: France. A considerable talent, he brought a delicate lyricism to his numerous scores for the cinema, above all those for Renoir (q.v.)*.

Main scores: *Le Crime de M. Lange* (co. Jean Wiener)*, *Jenny, Une Partie de campagne*, *La grande illusion*, *La Marseillaise*, *La Bête humaine*, *La Règle du jeu*, *Les Enfants du paradis, Les Portes de la nuit, Les Amants de Vérone, Juliette ou la clé des songes, Le Sang des bêtes, La Bergère et le ramoneur, Cela s'appelle l'aurore, Eléna et les hommes*, *Le Port du désir, Le Déjeuner sur l'herbe*, *Le huitième jour, Le Testament du Dr. Cordelier*, *Le Caporal épinglé*, *La Poupée, Les Moutons de Praxos, Le petit théâtre de Jean Renoir* (co. Jean WIENER).

237 KRUGER, Jules (1891 –). B: Strasbourg. Director of photography, best known during the Thirties.

Main films: *Napoléon* (co., 27), *L'Argent, La Fin du monde, Lac aux dames, La Bandera, La belle équipe, Pépé le Moko, Untel père et fils, Les Inconnus dans la maison.*

238 KURANT, Willy (1934 –). B: Liège. Director of photography who came to the fore thanks to his collaboration with Godard (q.v.), after working in Belgium and England.

Main films: *Masculin féminin, Les Créatures; Mon amour, mon amour; Trans-Europ-Express, Le Départ* (Skolimowski, Belgium, 67), *Une Histoire immortelle* (Welles, France, 68), *Night of the Following Day* (Cornfield, U.S.A., 68), *Le Temps de mourir, Cannabis.*

239 KYROU, Ado (1923 –). B: Athens. Greek director and writer. Since 1946: France. Author of several historical and critical studies: "Le Surréalisme au cinéma" (53), "Amour, Erotisme et Cinéma" (57), "Manuel du parfait petit spectateur" (58). His short films, often anarchistic and surrealist, include: *La Déroute* (57), *Le Palais idéal* (58), *Parfois le dimanche* (59), *Le Temps des assassins* (61), *Un honnête homme* (64). Feature: *Bloko* (shot in Greece but banned by the censors there, this dealt with an incident in the anti-Nazi resistance).

240 LACOMBE, Georges (1902 –   ). B: Paris. Director. Came to prominence in 1928 with a medium-length film on the slum suburbs of Paris, *La Zone*, a typical example of the socially committed *avant-garde* (q.v.) at the end of the Twenties. Lacombe later directed some first-rate commercial movies, including: *Les Musiciens du ciel, Le dernier des six, Le Pays sans étoiles, Martin Roumagnac, La Nuit est mon royaume.*

241 LAFONT, Bernadette (1938 –   ). B: Nîmes. Actress. At first dancer. Noted for her appearances in *Nouvelle Vague* films. Her gay, but unsophisticated frankness has been well used by Chabrol * and others.

Main films: *Les Mistons, Le beau Serge*, A double tour*, L'Eau à la bouche, Les bonnes femmes*, Les Godelureaux*, Et Satan conduit le bal, Tire-au-flanc, Le Voleur, Walls/Falak* (Kovács, Hungary, 68), *Un Idiot à Paris, Lamiel, La Fiancée du pirate, Piège, La Décharge; Valparaiso, Valparaiso; Les Stances à Sophie.*

242 LAI, Francis (1932 –   ). Composer. His score for *Une Homme et une femme* brought him international fame.

Main films: *Un Homme et une femme, Le*

Albert Lamorisse's FIFI LA PLUME

Soleil des voyous; Mon amour, mon amour; Vivre pour vivre, Un Idiot à Paris, La Leçon particulière, Mayerling (Young, France/Britain, 68), *Treize jours en France, Three into Two Won't Go* (Hall, Britain, 69); *La Vie, l'amour, la mort; Hannibal Brooks* (Winner, Britain, 69), *Un Homme qui me plaît, Le Voyou, Love Story* (Hiller, U.S.A., 70).

243 LAJOURNADE, Jean-Pierre (1937 –). B: Pau. Director. At first IDHEC (q.v.), then worked on TV series and shorts, including *Cinéma cinéma, Libre de ne pas l'être,* and *Le Droit d'asile* (69). A major figure of the aggressive and anarchist "third wave."

Films (also scripted): *Le Joueur de quilles, La Fin des Pyrénées.*

244 LAMORISSE, Albert (1922 – 1970). B: Paris. D: Teheran. Director. At first shorts, including *Bim le petit âne* (49), *Crin blanc* (52, which made his reputation), *Le Ballon rouge* (56). His work was tender, wistful, and more often lyrical than sentimental. He became identified with "Hélivision," whereby the camera was attached to a helicopter and swooped over landscapes and scenery.

Features: *Le Voyage en ballon, Fifi la plume.* Then, until his death in a flying accident during the shooting of *Le Vent des amoureux,* he concentrated on short documentaries and travel films, among them *Versailles* (67) and *Paris jamais vu* (68).

245 LANGLOIS, Henri (1914 –). B: Smyrna. A dedicated film enthusiast from his youth onwards, Langlois founded the *Cercle du Cinéma* (35) and then *La Cinémathèque française* (36, q.v.). He has helped to save innumerable films from destruction and has made them more widely known through the daily screenings he has arranged since 1945. He himself now has an international reputation and helps to promote elaborate film retrospectives all over the world.

246 LA PATELLIÈRE, Denys de (1921 –). B: Nantes. Director. At first assistant and short film specialist. Has made a great many competent films, most of them aimed at the big box-office.

Main films: *Les Aristocrates, Le Salaire du péché, Thérèse Etienne, Les grandes familles, Les Yeux de l'amour, Rue des Prairies, Un Taxi pour Tobrouk, Le Tonnerre de dieu, Le Voyage du père, Le Tatoué, Sabra.*

247 LAPOUJADE, Robert (1921 –). B: Montauban. Director. At first writer and painter. Turned to the cinema as a means of animating his pictures. 1959 – 67: a dozen cartoon shorts, among them *Foules, Prison, Vélodrame, Trois Portraits d'un oiseau qui n'existe pas, L'Ombre de la pomme.* In his first feature, *Le Socrate,* Lapoujade boldly combined live-action with animation with remarkable success. Then: *Le Sourire vertical.*

248 LAROCHE, Pierre (1902 – 1963). B. and D: Paris. Scriptwriter, respected for the quality of his scenarios and for his witty dialogue.

Main films: *Une Femme disparaît, Les Visiteurs du soir, Lumière d'été, L'Arche de Noé* (last three in collab. with Jacques Prévert, q.v.), *Clochemerle, L'étrange Madame X, Huis-clos, Cela s'appelle l'aurore, Le Monocle noir, Le septième juré.*

249 LAUTNER, Georges (1926 –). B: Nice. Director who has acquired a somewhat inflated reputation with his spy spoof films (the "Monocle" series).

Main films: *Arrêtez les tambours, Le Monocle noir, En plein cirage, Le septième juré, L'Oeil du monocle, Les Tontons flingueurs, Le Monocle rit jaune, Les Barbouzes, Galia, La grande sauterelle, La Route de Salina; Laisse aller, c'est une valse.*

250 LÉAUD, Jean-Pierre (1944 –). B: Paris. Actor. Discovered and launched by Truffaut (q.v.) while still a teenager, and later given a fresh impetus by Godard (also q.v.), Léaud has an impetuous and hilarious vitality that seems to express the youthful revolt of the Sixties.

Main films: *Les 400 coups, Le Testament d'Orphée, L'Amour à 20 ans* (Truffaut episode), *Masculin féminin, Le Père Noël a les yeux bleus, Made in USA, Le Départ* (Skolimowski, Belgium, 1967), *La Chinoise, Week-end, Le gai savoir, Baisers volés, Porcile* (Pasolini, Italy, 69), *Os herdeiros* (Diégues, 69), *Le Lion à sept têtes* (Rocha, 70), *Domicile conjugal, Une Aventure de Billy le Kid.*

251 LE CHANOIS, Jean-Paul (1909 –). B: Paris. Director. At first actor, notably in *L'Affaire est dans le sac* (under his real name, Jean-Paul Dreyfus), and scriptwriter. Most of his work has been socially committed, in a very sentimental fashion.

Main films: *Au cœur de l'orage, L'Ecole buissonnière, Sans laisser d'adresse, Agence matrimoniale; Papa, Maman, la bonne et moi; Papa, Maman, ma femme et moi; Le Cas du Dr. Laurent, Les Misérables, Monsieur.*

252 LEENHARDT, Roger (1903 –). B: Paris. Director. From the late Thirties onwards, Leenhardt was an excellent film critic. He has made several outstanding documentaries, including *Naissance du cinéma* (46), *Victor Hugo* (51), *François Mauriac* (55), *J.-J. Rousseau* (57), *Paul Valéry* (60). Features: *Les dernières vacances, Le Rendez-vous de minuit.* Latterly he has returned to the documentary and biographical films that are his *forte.*

Jean-Pierre Léaud in LES 400 COUPS

253 LÉGER, Fernand (1881 – 1955). B: Argentan. D: Paris. Painter and *cinéaste*, a member of the *avant-garde* (q.v.) in the Twenties.

Films: *Charlot cubiste* (unfinished cartoon, 21), *Le Ballet mécanique* (medium length), *Dreams that Money Can Buy* (portmanteau film supervised by Hans Richter, one episode, 44).

254 LEGRAND, Michel (1932 –   ). B: Paris. Orchestral leader, composer, and song writer. 1944: first prize at the Conservatoire. His score for *Les Parapluies de Cherbourg* made him world famous. His style is both lyrical and dynamic.

Main films: *L'Amérique insolite, Lola, Terrain vague, Un Cœur gros comme ça, Cléo de 5 à 7, Une femme est une femme, La Baie des Anges, Le joli Mai, Bande à part, Les Parapluies de Cherbourg, La Vie de château, Les Demoiselles de Rochefort, Qui êtes-vous Polly Maggoo?, The Thomas Crown Affair* (Jewison, U.S.A., 68), *Play Dirty* (De Toth, Britain, 68), *Ice Station Zebra* (John Sturges, U.S.A., 69), *Castle Keep* (Pollack, U.S.A., 69), *La Piscine, The Happy Ending* (Brooks, U.S.A., 69), *Pieces of Dreams* (Haller, U.S.A., 70), *Peau d'âne.*

255 LELOUCH, Claude (1937 –   ). B: Paris. Director. At first advertising films and

Claude Lelouch

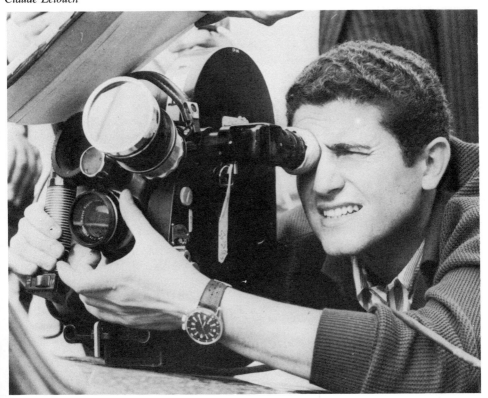

shorts, including *Le Rideau se lève* and *La Jungle de Paris*, both 57. The enormous international success of *Un Homme et une femme* made Lelouch, with Godard (q.v.), the most well-known of French directors. He is a talented technician, but his handling of "big" themes remains infuriatingly superficial. Also produced and photographed several of his films.

Films: *Le Propre de l'homme, L'Amour avec des si, La Femme spectacle, Une Fille et des fusils, Les grands moments, Un Homme et une femme, Vivre pour vivre, Loin du Vietnam* (one episode), *Treize jours en France* (co.-dir. François Reichenbach); *La Vie, l'amour, la mort; Un Homme qui me plaît, Le Voyou.* Also producer ("Les Films 13"): *Le Mur, Sept jours ailleurs, Les Gauloises bleues, L'Indiscret, Benito Cereno* etc.

256 LEROI, Francis (1946 –   ). Director. A typical representative of the latest film generation, with his spontaneity and disrespect for the traditional roles of visual expression.

Films: *Pop Game, Ciné Girl, La Poupée rouge.*

257 LÉVY, Raoul J. (1922 – 1966). B: Antwerp. D: Saint-Tropez. Producer and director. Committed suicide after a fruitful career that ended with a financial disaster (*Marco Polo*, 62, never finished).

Main films (as producer): *Les Orgueilleux, Et Dieu créa la femme, Pardonnez nos offenses, Sait-on jamais, Les Bijoutiers du clair de lune, En cas de malheur, Babette s'en va-t-en guerre, Moderato cantabile, La Vérité, Deux ou trois choses que je sais d'elle.* As director: *Je vous salue Mafia, L'Espion.*

258 L'HERBIER, Marcel (1890 –   ). B: Paris. Prominent director of the *avant-garde* (q.v.) during the Twenties. After playing a significant part in improving the range of film expression, L'Herbier turned to mainly commercial productions. 1943: founded IDHEC (q.v.). 1953: becomes TV producer.

Main films: *Phantasmes, Rose France, Le Carnival des vérités, L'Homme du large, Eldorado, Don Juan et Faust, L'Inhumaine, Feu Mathias Pascal, L'Argent, La Tragédie impériale, Entente cordiale, La Comédie du bonheur, La Nuit fantastique, Les derniers jours de Pompéi.*

259 LINDER, Max (1883 – 1925). B: Saint-Loubès. D: Paris. Famous comedian. Directed, scripted, and acted in several hundred shorts and some features. Under the name of "Max," he created a clumsy and sympathetic "dandy" figure whose influence Chaplin acknowledged. 1917 and 1921 – 22: U.S.A.

Features: *Sept ans de malheur, Soyez ma femme, L'étroit mousquetaire* (all U.S.A.), *Le Roi du cirque* (in Austria). *En compagnie de Max Linder*, an anthology of his films, was compiled by his daughter Maud Linder in 1963.

260 LODS, Jean (1903 –   ). Director. Specialist in documentary shorts and art films, whose work is warm, talented, and observant.

Main films: *Le Mile* (32), *La Vie d'un fleuve, la Seine* (33), *Aristide Maillol, sculpteur* (43), *Aubusson et Jean Lurçat* (46), *Hommage à Albert Einstein* (55), *Henri Barbusse* (58), *Jean Jaurès* (59), *Stéphane Mallarmé* (60). 1945 – 52: head of IDHEC (q.v.).

261 LOTAR, Éli (1905 – 1969). B: Paris. Director and director of photography. At first stills photographer, then camera operator on a number of documentaries, including *Zuiderzee* (Ivens, 29) and *Las Hurdes* (Buñuel, 32). Directed a superbly lyrical and socially committed documentary, *Aubervilliers* (with songs by Prévert and Kosma, 45).

262 LOURIÉ, Eugène (1905 –   ). B: Russia. Since 1921: France. Well-known set

Max Linder in SEPT ANS DE MALHEUR

designer, closely associated with Renoir * (q.v.).

Main films (as art director): *Crime et châtiment, Les Bas-fonds*, La grande illusion*, L'Alibi, La Bête humaine*, Sans lendemain, La Règle du jeu*, The Southerner*, Diary of a Chambermaid*, The River*, Limelight* (Chaplin, Britain, 53). Settled in the U.S.A. since 1940, he has directed some interesting science fiction films, including *The Beast from 20,000 Fathoms* (52), *The Colossus of New York* (57), *Gorgo* (60).

263 LUMIÈRE, Louis (1864 – 1948). B: Besançon. D: Bandol. With his brother **Auguste** (1862 – 1954), he invented the *Cinématographe* (1895). The simple and practical features of their equipment enabled the Lumières to distribute it throughout the world in a short time. Louis directed several hundred short documentaries and sent cameramen to many different countries. Some of his most famous titles (all 1895): *La Sortie des usines, L'Arroseur arrosé, Le Déjeuner de bébé, Arrivée d'un train en gare de La Ciotat, Barque sortant du port, Partie d'écarté, Démolition d'un mur.*

264 LUNTZ, Édouard (1931 –). B: La Baule. Director. At first assistant to Nicholas Ray, Jean Grémillon and others. Then some outspoken and incisive shorts, including *Enfants des courants d'air* (Prix Vigo, 60), *Bon pour le service* (62). Luntz's work is unusual (and strongly critical of society).

Films: *Les Cœurs verts* (also scripted), *Le Grabuge* (produced by Fox-France, who refused to release it), *Le dernier saut, L'Humeur vagabonde.*

265 MAGNE, Michel (1930–). Composer. Some skilled work for concert recitals, then more commercial music for films.

Main scores: *Le Vice et la vertu, Le Repos du guerrier, Symphonie pour un massacre, Le Monocle rit jaune, Mélodie en sous-sol, Germinal, Cyrano et d'Artagnan, Le Journal d'une femme en blanc, Compartiment tueurs, A Cœur joie, Barbarella.*

266 MALLE, Louis (1932–). B: Thumeries. Director. 1952–53: IDHEC. At first assistant to Bresson, q.v. Began his career a little ahead of most *Nouvelle Vague* directors, and became internationally famous with *Les Amants.* A major film-maker whose work has been classically elegant in style, although recently he has leaned towards the docu-

Above: Louis Malle. Below: Philippe Noiret, Catherine Demongeot and Carla Marlier in Malle's
ZAZIE DANS LE MÉTRO

At right: Jean Marais. Above: André Malraux's ESPOIR

mentary. Also TV work. Acted: *La Voie lactée, La Fiancée du pirate.*

Films: *Le Monde du silence* (co.-dir. J.-Y. Cousteau), *Ascenseur pour l'échafaud, Les Amants, Zazie dans le métro, Vie privée, Le Feu follet, Viva Maria, Le Voleur, Histoires extraordinaires* (*William Wilson* episode), *Calcutta* (doc.), *Le Souffle au cœur.*

267 MALRAUX, André (1901 –). B: Paris. Novelist. Directed one profoundly lyrical film, based on his own novel: *Espoir (Sierra de Teruel)*. Also wrote an interesting film book: "Esquisse d'une psychologie du cinéma" (46).

268 MARAIS, Jean (1913 –). B: Cherbourg. Stage and screen actor. At first photographer. Very popular leading man and the French cinema's Don Juan during the Forties

and Fifties. Close collaboration with Cocteau (q.v.) *.

Main films: *L'éternel retour*, *La Belle et la bête*, *Ruy Blas, L'Aigle à deux têtes*, *Les Parents terribles*, *Orphée*, *Le Château de verre, Napoléon* (54), *Eléna et les hommes, SOS Noronha, Typhon sur Nagasaki, Un Amour de poche, Le Testament d'Orphée*, *Austerlitz, La Princesse de Clèves, Fantômas, Peau d'âne*.

269 MARCHAL, Georges (1920 –   ). B: Nancy. Actor, at first "jeune premier," then a more mature and dependable personality.

Main films: *Lumière d'été, Si Versailles m'était conté, Cela s'appelle l'aurore, La Mort en ce jardin, Austerlitz, Belle de jour, La Voie lactée*.

Josette Day and Jean Marais in LA BELLE ET LA BÊTE

The Algerian in Marker's LE JOLI MAI

270 MAREY, Étienne-Jules (1830 – 1904).
B: Beaune. D: Paris. Doctor, scientist, and
inventor. The discovery of photography gave
Marey the idea of printing the different stages
of a movement in order to reconstitute it by
running one image after another on a band of
film. He invented the *Fusil photographique*
(photo-gun) to record specific movements. His
Chronophotographe, developed in 1890, was
the immediate precursor of the Lumière
Cinématographe.

271 MARKER, Chris (1921 –   ). RN:
Christian François Bouche-Villeneuve. Photographer and director. One of the more diverting
figures of the *Nouvelle Vague*, whose output has
consisted almost exclusively of *cinéma-vérité*
(q.v.). His films, usually short or medium
length, are very human, lucid, and acutely
intelligent documentaries. Assisted Resnais
(q.v.) on *Nuit et brouillard*.

Films: *Olympia 52* (52), *Les Statues meurent
aussi* (co.-dir. Resnais, 52), *Dimanche à Pékin*
(56), *Lettre de Sibérie* (58), *Les Astronautes*
(co.-dir. Walerian Borowczyk), *Description
d'un combat* (60), *Cuba si!* (61), *La Jetée* (62),
Le joli Mai (full-length doc.), *A Valparaiso*
(editing only), *La Brûlure de mille soleils*
(editing only), *Le Mystère Koumiko* (65), *Si
j'avais quatre dromadaires* (full-length photo-

montage, 66), *Loin du Vietnam* (collab.), *La sixième face du Pentagone* (68), *A bientôt j'espère* (co. Mario Marret, 68), *La Bataille des dix millions* (70).

272 MATÉ, Rudolph (1898 – 1964). B: Cracow. D: Hollywood. Director and director of photography. Polish by birth, he worked in France 1921 – 35 and shot several notable films, among them *La Passion de Jeanne d'Arc* and *Vampyr* (for Dreyer), *Dans les rues* (Trivas), *Le dernier milliardaire* (Clair), *Liliom* (Lang). Later he became a major cinematographer in Hollywood, especially on *The Flame of New Orleans* (Clair). From 1948: directed films in his own right.

273 MATRAS, Christian (1903 –). B: Valence, Drôme. Director of photography, respected for the fluidity and grace of his work. At first reporter for Eclair-Journal, then camera assistant. Long collab. with Ophuls *.

Main films: *L'Or des mers, La grande illusion, Entrée des artistes, La Fin du jour, Le dernier tournant, La Duchesse de Langeais, Boule de suif, L'Idiot, L'Aigle à deux têtes, La Ronde*, Le Plaisir** (two episodes), *Fanfan la Tulipe, Madame de . . .*, Lola Montès*, Les Espions, Montparnasse 19, Le Cœur battant, Thérèse Desqueyroux, Cartouche, Les Fêtes galantes, Les Oiseaux vont mourir au Pérou, La Voie lactée, Le Bal du Comte d'Orgel.*

274 MAYO (1905 –). B: Port Said. Costume designer and art director, whose work for the cinema has been infrequent but outstanding.

Main films: *Les Enfants du paradis, Les Portes de la nuit, La Beauté du diable, Juliette ou la Clé des songes, Casque d'or, Le Rideau cramoisi, Mina de Vanghel, Une Vie, Amélie ou le temps d'aimer, Léviathan.*

275 MEDVECZKY, Diourka (1930 –). Director. Born in Hungary, and a sculptor

by profession. In his spare time he has created a body of films shot through with violence and poetry. Shorts: *Marie et le curé* (66), *Jeanne et la moto* (68).

Feature: *Paul.*

276 MEERSON, Lazare (1900 – 1938). B: Russia. D: London. Set designer of considerable talent, whose premature death was a tragedy for the cinema. 1924: came to France. He brought together in his *décors* the Russian constructivism of his youth and the German expressionism of the Twenties, to arrive at an extremely personal and distinctive style.

Main films: *Feu Mathias Pascal* (in collab. with Cavalcanti), *Carmen, L'Argent, La Proie du vent* (co.), *Un Chapeau de paille d'Italie, Les deux timides, Sous les toits de Paris, Le Million, A nous la liberté, Quatorze Juillet, Ciboulette, Le grand jeu, Lac aux dames, Pension Mimosas, La Kermesse héroïque.* From 1936, in England: *Break the News, Knight without Armour.*

277 MÉLIÈS, Georges (1861 – 1938). B: Paris. D: Orly. Director. The great pioneer of the fictional film, just as Lumière (q.v.) was the pioneer of the documentary film. At first cartoonist, conjuror, and director of the Robert Houdin theatre, Méliès is rightly considered as the inventor of the film as a *spectacle* because he brought to the cinema all the visual and dramatic devices associated with magic and fantasy. He developed nearly all the cinema's special effects, and used them with wit and sensitivity. Between 1896 and 1913 he made several hundred shorts.

Main films: *Une Partie de cartes* (96), *Bombardement d'une maison* (97), *Illusions fantasmagoriques, Guillaume Tell, L'Homme de têtes* (98), *Le Christ marchant sur les eaux, L'Affaire Dreyfus, Cendrillon, L'Homme-Protée* (99), *Jeanne d'Arc, Rêves de Noël* (1900), *Le petit chaperon rouge, Barbe-Bleue* (01), *L'Homme à la tête de caoutchouc, L'Œuf*

Above: *L'HOMME À LA TÊTE DE CAOUTCHOUC.* *Below:* *LE VOYAGE DANS LA LUNE*

magique prolifique, Le Voyage dans le lune, Voyages de Gulliver, Robinson Crusoe (02), *Cake-walk infernal, Le Royaume des fées, La Damnation de Faust* (03), *Le merveilleux éventail vivant* (04), *Le Palais des mille et une nuits* (05), *Jack le ramoneur, Les incendiaires, Les quatre cents farces du Diable, Robert Macaire et Bertrand* (06), *Deux cent mille lieues sous les mers, Le Tunnel sous la Manche* (07), *La Civilisation à travers les âges, Le Raid New York-Paris en automobile* (08), *Les Aventures du baron Munchhausen* (11), *A la conquête du Pôle* (his masterpiece, 12).

278 MELVILLE, Jean-Pierre (1917 –   ). B: Paris. Director. At first worked in business. Spent Second World War in England. Played an important part as the early predecessor of the *Nouvelle Vague* (q.v.) with his first feature,

Le Silence de la mer, based on the novel by Vercors. A precise director who studies human relationships in an atmosphere of dramatic intensity (crime, war, etc.). Acted: *Orphée, A bout de souffle, Zazie dans le métro, Un Amour de poche, Landru,* and *Deux Hommes dans Manhattan.* Scripted or co-scripted * most of his films.

Films: *Vingt-quatre heures dans la vie d'un clown* (short, 45), *Le Silence de la mer*, *Les Enfants terribles*, *Quand tu liras cette lettre, Bob le Flambeur*, *Deux Hommes dans Manhattan*; *Léon Morin, prêtre*; *Le Doulos*, *L'Aîné des Ferchaux*, *Le deuxième souffle*, *Le Samouraï*, *L'Armée des ombres*, *Le Cercle rouge*.

279 MESGUISCH, Félix (1871 – 1949). B: Algiers. Newsreel cameraman, one of the

Alain Delon and Jean-Pierre Melville at work on LE CERCLE ROUGE

Francis Blanche and Bourvil in Jean-Pierre Mocky's UN DRÔLE DE PAROISSIEN

first in the field (from 1895 onwards). He toured the world on behalf of the Lumière brothers and brought back hundreds of thousands of feet of film that constitute a unique and perceptive record of all kinds of people and places.

280 MEURISSE, Paul (1912–). B: Dunkerque. Stage and screen actor, noted for his dramatic power and wry sense of humour. At first cabaret in Marseille. 1941: enters cinema.

Main films: *Macadam, Les Diaboliques, La Tête contre les murs, Marie-Octobre, Le Déjeuner sur l'herbe, Les nouveaux aristocrates, La Vérité, Du Mouron pour les petits oiseaux, Le Monocle noir, Le Monocle rit jaune, L'Œil du monocle, Quand passent les faisans, Le deuxième souffle, L'Armée des ombres, Le Cri du cormoran le soir au-dessus des jonques, Doucement les basses.*

281 MOCKY, Jean-Pierre (1929–). B: Nice. Director. At first actor. Main films as actor: *Orphée, Dieu a besoin des hommes, I vinti* (Antonioni, Italy, 52), *Gli sbandati* (Maselli, Italy, 55), *La Tête contre les murs* (also co-scripted), and many of his own films. Directs with a blend of black humour and fierce aggression.

Films (also co-scripted): *Les Dragueurs, Un Couple, Snobs, Les Vierges, Un drôle de paroissien, La Cité de l'indicible peur/La grande frousse, La Bourse et la vie, Les Compagnons de la marguerite, La grande lessive, Solo, L'Etalon, L'Albatros.*

282 MODOT, Gaston (1887–1970). B: Paris. Actor. His tall, stern figure was familiar to filmgoers for over half a century.

Main films: the *Onésime* series (starting in 1908), *La Fête espagnole, Fièvre, Sous les toits* de Paris, *L'Age d'or*, *Die Dreigroschenoper* (Pabst, Germany, 31), *Quatorze Juillet*, *La Bandera*, *Pépé le Moko*, *La grande illusion*, *La Marseillaise*, *La Règle du jeu*, *Dernier atout*, *Les Enfants du paradis*, *Le Silence est d'or*, *Antoine et Antoinette*, *Casque d'or*, *La Beauté du diable*, *French Cancan*, *Cela s'appelle l'aurore*, *Les Amants*, *Le Testament du Dr. Cordelier*. Modot directed one extraordinary medium-length film: *La Torture par l'espérance* (28).

283 MOLINARO, Édouard (1928 –   ). B: Bordeaux. Director. After a promising start, his career has been mainly concerned with rather colourless commercial productions.

Films (also scripted *): *Le Dos au mur*, *Des Femmes disparaissent*, *Un Témoin dans la ville**, *Une Fille pour l'été**, *La Mort de Belle*, *Les Ennemis**, *Les sept péchés capitaux* (*L'Envie* episode), *Arsène Lupin contre Arsène Lupin*, *Une ravissante idiote**, *Chasse à l'homme*, *Quand passant les faisans*, *Peau d'espion**, *Oscar**, *Hibernatus*, *La Liberté en croupe*, *Les Aveux les plus doux*.

284 MONTAND, Yves (1921 –   ). B: Venice. RN: Ivo Livi. Actor. Since 1924: France. A useful light comedian in the Forties, Montand has recently come into a second and more serious phase of his career. Also a successful singer.

Main films: *Etoile sans lumière*, *Les Portes de la nuit*, *Souvenirs perdus*, *Le Salaire de la peur*, *Napoléon* (54), *Marguerite de la nuit*, *Les Sorcières de Salem*, *Let's Make Love* (Cukor, U.S.A., 60), *Sanctuary* (Richardson, U.S.A., 60), *Compartiment tueurs*, *La Guerre est finie*, *Paris brûle-t-il?*, *Grand Prix* (Frankenheimer, U.S.A., 66), *Vivre pour vivre*; *Un Soir, un train*

Yves Montand in LE CERCLE ROUGE

Jean-Claude Brialy and Jeanne Moreau in LA MARIÉE ÉTAIT EN NOIR

(Delvaux, Belgium, 68), *Mr. Freedom, Le Diable par la queue, Z, L'Aveu, On a Clear Day You Can See Forever* (Minnelli, U.S.A., 70), *Le Cercle rouge, La Folie des grandeurs.*

285 MOREAU, Jeanne (1928–). B: Paris. Stage and screen actress. Also singer. Attended the Conservatoire, then at Comédie-Française and the TNP. One of the most respected stars in the French cinema, grave or gay as a part demands, and always projecting sophistication allied to sensuality. 1949: *début* in cinema.

Main films: *Touchez pas au grisbi, Le Salaire du péché, Ascenseur pour l'échafaud, Le Dos au mur, Les Amants, Les Liaisons dangereuses, Le Dialogue des Carmélites, Five Branded Women* (Ritt, Italy, 60), *Moderato Cantabile* (Brook, France, 60), *La notte* (Antonioni, Italy, 60), *Jules et Jim, Eva* (Losey, Italy, 61), *Le Procès* (Welles, France/Italy/West Germany, 62). *La Baie des Anges, The Victors* (Foreman, Britain, 63), *Le Feu follet, Peau de banane, Le Journal d'une femme de chambre, The Train* (Frankenheimer, U.S.A., 64); *Mata Hari, Agent H 21; The Yellow Rolls-Royce* (Asquith, Britain, 65), *Viva Maria, Mademoiselle* (Richardson, France/Britain, 66), *Chimes at Midnight* (Welles, Spain/Switzerland, 66), *The Sailor from Gibraltar* (Richard-

son, Britain, 66), *La Mariée était en noir, Le plus vieux métier du monde* (one episode), *Une Histoire immortelle* (Welles, France, 68), *Great Catherine* (Flemyng, Britain, 68), *Le Corps de Diane, Monte Walsh* (Fraker, U.S.A., 70), *Alex in Wonderland* (Mazursky, U.S.A., 71), *Comptes à rebours, Mille Baisers de Florence*.

286 MORENO, Marguerite (1871 – 1948). B: Paris. D: Touzac. Stage and screen actress. One of the most dazzling and witty stars of the prewar period.

Main films: *Les Misérables, Le Roman d'un tricheur, Ces dames aux chapeaux verts, Les Perles de la couronne, Regain, Ils étaient neuf célibataires, Douce, Un Revenant, L'Idiot, Les Jeux sont faits*.

287 MORGAN, Michèle (1920 –). B: Neuilly. RN: Simone Roussel. Actress. Made famous by Carné (q.v.) as the doom-laden heroine of *Quai des brumes*, and maturing subsequently into an attractive and elegant "grande dame." A top box-office attraction since the Fifties. 1940 – 46: U.S.A. Also singer.

Main films: *Gribouille, Orage, Quai des brumes, La Loi du Nord, Remorques, Untel père et fils, La Symphonie pastorale, The Fallen Idol* (Reed, Britain, 48), *Aux Yeux du souvenir, La Château de verre, La Minute de vérité, Les Orgueilleux, Napoléon* (54), *Les grandes manœuvres, Marguerite de la nuit, Si Paris nous était conté, Le Miroir à deux faces, Fortunat, Le Crime ne paie pas, Lost Command* (Robson, U.S.A., 65), *Landru, Benjamin*.

288 MOULLET, Luc (1941 –). B: St. Cyrice (Seine). Director. At first critic (*Cahiers du Cinéma*) and short film-maker (*Un Steak trop cuit*, 60; *Terres noires*, 61, etc.). His work has a strong vein of satire.

Films: *Brigitte et Brigitte, Les Contrebandières, Une Aventure de Billy le Kid*.

289 MOUSSINAC, Léon (1890 – 1964). B: Laroche-Migennes. D: Paris. Film theorist. One of the pioneers of serious film criticism, whose work was exceptionally intelligent and lucid. Also a specialist in theatre history. Head of IDHEC (1947 – 49), and then of the National School for Decorative Arts.

Main books: "Naissance du cinéma" (25), "Le Cinéma soviétique" (28), "Panoramique du cinéma" (29), "L'Age ingrat du cinéma" (46), "Sergei Eisenstein" (64).

290 MOUSSY, Marcel (1924–). B: Algiers. Scriptwriter. Also novelist. Became known for his collaboration with *Nouvelle Vague* directors.

Main films (as scriptwriter): *Les 400 coups, Tirez sur le pianiste, La Sentence, Ballade pour un voyou, Fahrenheit 451*. As director: some shorts, then two features, *Saint-Tropez Blues, Trois hommes sur un cheval*.

291 MUSIDORA (1889–1957). B. and D: Paris. RN: Jeanne Roques. Actress. The French cinema's first, and most famous, *vamp*. Her black-clad presence is one of the most bizarre and enduring images of the Feuillade serials. She made several films between 1915 and 1925 but never achieved the success she did in *Les Vampires* and *Judex*. From 1930: journalist. Later did research for the *Cinémathèque française* (q.v.).

292 NAT, Marie-José (1940–). B: Bonifacio. Actress. Poised and distinguished brunette. Married to Michel Drach (q.v.).

Main films: *Crime et châtiment* (56), *Rue des Prairies, La Française et l'amour, La Vérité, Amélie ou le temps d'aimer, Education sentimentale, Les sept péchés capitaux, La Vie conjugale, Journal d'une femme en blanc, Elise ou la vraie vie*.

293 NATURALISM. Term used to describe a stylistic and thematic trend referring to the literary and theatrical school of the period 1870–90. The writings of Zola and Maupassant and, on stage, the productions of André Antoine (q.v.), are typical of the desire for realism and objectivity that marked this trend. It can also be found in the *vérisme* of the Italian novelist Giovanni Verga. In the cinema, naturalism in its early stages coloured several Zola adaptations, then the films of Feuillade and André Antoine (qq.v.).

During the Thirties, at a time when the *réalisme poétique* school (q.v.) was predominant, the naturalist trend appeared side by side or even simultaneously in the work of Carné, Feyder, and Duvivier (qq.v.). After the war, naturalism was again in vogue with directors like Clément, Clouzot, Yves Allégret, and Autant-Lara (qq.v.).

In terms of style, naturalism rejects the charming and the picturesque while relying to some extent on expressionist lighting. In terms of subject matter, it resorts to ugly, violent, and pessimistic themes, even when describing authentic social conditions (*Un Homme marche dans la ville*). It is in effect an extreme and frustrated form of realism.

294 NOIRET, Philippe (1931–). B: Lille. Stage and screen actor, also cabaret artist. Heavily-built supporting player who has become a star thanks to his wit and cheerful *bonhomie*.

Main films: *La Pointe courte, Zazie dans le métro, Tout l'or du monde, Cyrano et d'Artagnan, Thérèse Desqueyroux, Ballade pour un voyou, Monsieur, Les Copains, Night of the Generals* (Litvak, France/Britain, 66), *La Vie de château, Qui êtes-vous Polly Maggoo?, L'Une et l'autre, Alexandre le bienheureux, Mr. Freedom, Justine* (Cukor, U.S.A., 68), *Topaz* (Hitchcock, U.S.A., 69), *Clérambard, L'Etalon, Murphy's War* (Yates, U.S.A., 70), *Les Aveux les plus doux*.

295 NOUVELLE VAGUE ("New Wave"). Term invented by the press to describe the renaissance in French cinema from about 1958 to 1961, and the group of young directors associated with the movement.

Chabrol (q.v.) was the forerunner of the *Nouvelle Vague,* making his first feature, *Le beau Serge,* outside the normal production system. He was soon followed by Rivette, Truffaut, Godard, Resnais, Demy, Malle, Doniol-Valcroze (qq.v.) etc. Various other directors had prepared the ground for this explosion of talent. Melville (q.v.) with *Le Silence de la mer* (48), produced more or less independently; Astruc (q.v.) with *Le Rideau cramoisi* (52); Varda (q.v.) with *La Pointe courte* (54): these three films were linked by a deliberate use of interior monologue and revealed the typical *Nouvelle Vague* fondness for psychological analysis. With *Et Dieu créa la femme* (56), Vadim (q.v.) was the first to launch an attack on established moral taboos.

On the theoretical side, there were two key texts: Astruc's *caméra-stylo* manifesto (q.v.), and Truffaut's article "Une certaine tendance du cinéma français" (54), in which he violently criticised the worn-out format of "Papa's cinema," symbolised by the films of Delannoy (q.v.). Strictly speaking, the *Nouvelle Vague* ended around 1962; one can argue that a "second wave" then appeared, led by such men as Allio, Jessua, Herman, Luntz, Lelouch, Moullet (qq.v.) etc., and a third one a little later, with Garrel, Karmitz, Lajournade, Leroi, Varela etc.

Below: Sylvia Monfort and Philippe Noiret in LA POINTE COURTE. Page 97: Jean-Paul Belmondo (symbol of the Nouvelle Vague*) in Godard's À BOUT DE SOUFFLE*

Jean-Luc Godard's PIERROT LE FOU. Jean-Paul Belmondo with Anna Karina in one of the most controversial films of the Sixties. Photo: Rome Paris Films.

Malle's VIVA MARIA. Jeanne Moreau under fire in
the Mexican revolution.

Above: Bulle Ogier and Pierre Clémenti in LES IDOLES. Below: Max Ophuls. Opposite: Ophuls's
LOLA MONTÈS

296 OGIER, Bulle (1939 –   ). Actress. An outstanding discovery of recent years— graceful, delicate, and inspiring.

Films: *Les Idoles, L'Amour fou, Pierre et Paul, 48h. d'amour, Paulina s'en va, Les Stances à Sophie, Out One, Rendez-vous à Braye* (A. Delvaux, 71).

297 OPHULS, Marcel (1927 –   ). B: Frankfurt. Director. Son of Max Ophuls. After a worthy *début*, this young director has not really fulfilled his promise. Also made a first-class short, *Matisse ou le talent du bonheur*.

Films: *L'Amour à vingt ans* (one episode), *Peau de banane, Feu à volonté, Le Chagrin et la pitié* (TV doc.).

298 OPHULS, Max (1902 – 1957). B: Saarbrücken. D: Hamburg. RN: Max Oppen-

heimer. Director. At first actor, then stage producer up to 1932. German-born, he worked part of his life in France (1933 – 41 and 1950 – 57), as well as Italy and the U.S.A. A great romantic director whose films are distinguished by their marvellous fluidity and enchanting atmosphere.

Films in France: *Une Histoire d'amour, On a volé un homme, Divine, La tendre ennemie, Yoshiwara, Werther, Sans lendemain, De Mayerling à Sarajevo, La Ronde, Le Plaisir, Madame de . . ., Lola Montès.*

299 O R A I N, Fred (1909 –). B: Bonnemain. Producer. Important not so much for the number of films he has produced as for the influence he wields in the profession and the amount of responsibility he has assumed on the technical and labour side of the industry. Produced several shorts and some features, including *Jour de fête, Premières armes, Les Vacances de M. Hulot.*

300 O U R Y, Gérard (1919 –). B: Paris. RN: Max-Gérard Houry Tannenbaum. Actor and director. 1939: stage *début*. Second World War: in Switzerland. Stage work in Geneva.

Main films (as actor): *Antoine et Antoinette, La Nuit est mon royaume, Les Héros sont fatigués, La meilleure part, Le Dos au mur*. As director (all competent box-office successes): *La Main chaude, La Menace, Le Crime ne paie pas, Le Corniaud, La grande vadrouille, Le Cerveau, La Folie des grandeurs.*

301 P A G E, Louis (1905 –). B: Lyon. Director of photography. At first assistant to Périnal, Thirard, and Schuftan (qq.v.). Assistant director to Cocteau on *Le Sang d'un poète* (30). His realistic style made him a much sought-after lighting cameraman during the Forties. Towards the end of his career he worked on several Jean Gabin pictures *.

Main films: *Espoir, Lumière d'été, Le Ciel est à vous, Le Pays sans étoiles, Le 6 Juin à l'aube* (co.), *Macadam, Au-delà des grilles*, L'étrange Madame X, L'Amour d'une femme, En effeuillant la marguerite, Les grandes familles*, Le Baron de l'Ecluse*, Le Président*, Les Vieux de la vieille*, Un Singe en hiver*, Mélodie en soussol*, Monsieur*.*

302 P A G L I E R O, Marcel (1907 –). B: London. Italian actor and director who worked for a time in France. Numerous acting appearances, including *Les Jeux sont faits, Dédée d'Anvers, Le bel âge, Les mauvais coups.*

Films (as director only): *Un Homme marche dans la ville, Les Amants de Bras-mort, La Rose rouge, La Putain respecteuse.*

303 P A G N O L, Marcel (1895 –). B: Aubagne, Bouches-du-Rhône. Director. At first successful dramatist. 1932: founded a production company in order to film his own plays and thus reach a mass public. Inspired by the inhabitants and landscape of the Midi, his work has enjoyed considerable popularity. His first two adaptations were directed by Alexander Korda (*Marius*) and Marc Allégret (*Fanny*). Pagnol scripted *Tartarin de Tarascon, Le Rosier de Madame Husson*, and all his own films. The first *cinéaste* to be admitted to the *Académie française*. Pagnol has written several autobiographical books, "Souvenirs d'enfance" (1957 – 60).

Films (as director): *Topaze, Direct au cœur Le Gendre de M. Poirier, Léopold le bien-aimé Angèle, Merlusse, Cigalon, César, Regain, Le Schpountz, La Femme du boulanger, La Fille du puisatier, Naïs, La belle Meunière, Topaze* (51). *Manon des sources, Les Lettres de mon moulin*

304 P A I N L E V É, Jean (1902 –). B: Paris. Director of shorts, specialising in scientific documentaries. 1930: founded the Institut de Cinéma scientifique. Several of his shorts are works of art over and above their scientific interest.

Raimu in Marcel Pagnol's LA FEMME DU BOULANGER

Main films: *La Pieuvre* (28), *Les Oursins* (29), *Les Crabes* (30), *L'Hippocampe* (34), *Voyage dans le ciel* (37), *Images mathématiques de la 4ème dimension* (37), *Le Vampire* (45), *Assassins d'eau douce* (47), *Ecriture de la danse* (48), *Les Danseurs de la mer* (60), etc.

305 PANIJEL, Jacques (1921 –   ). B: Paris. Director. At first novelist and dramatic adviser.

Films: *La Peau et les os* (co.-dir. Jean-Paul Sassy), *Octobre à Paris* (feature-length documentary shot anonymously and in secret on the violent French police tactics mounted against the Arabs at the time of the Algerian war).

306 PATHÉ, Charles (1863 – 1957). B: Chevry-Cossigny. D: Monte Carlo. Founded, with his three brothers in 1896, the firm "Pathé

Frères," which rapidly developed into France's (and the world's) largest manufacturer of film equipment as well as producing films. His enormous empire was split up and sold in 1918 when the French cinema, affected by the economic crisis, lost its premier status in Europe. Pathé had opened branches in several countries, started the first regular newsreel ("Pathé Gazette" 1910), and launched the work of many directors (including Zecca, q.v.) and actors (Max Linder, q.v., André Deed, known as Boireau, and Prince Rigadin). Has written two books of memoirs: "Souvenirs et conseils d'un parvenu" (1926), and "De Pathé-Frères à Pathé-Cinéma" (1940).

307 PAUL, Bernard (1930 –   ). Director. Married to Françoise ARNOUL. At first assistant. His one film to date, *Le Temps de*

Jean Grémillon's LUMIÈRE D'ETÉ, produced by André Paulvé

Jeanne Valérie and Gérard Philipe in LES LIAISONS DANGEREUSES

vivre, shows an interesting approach to social problems.

308 PAULVÉ, André (1898 –). B: Seignelay. Producer, known for some important films, including *Lumière d'été, Les Visiteurs du soir, L'éternel retour, Sylvie et le fantôme, La Belle et la bête, Les Maudits, La Chartreuse de Parme, Orphée, Casque d'or.*

309 PAVIOT, Paul (1926 –). B: Paris. Director. At first photographer, then short and medium-length films, including *Terreur en Oklahoma* (50), *Chicago Digest* (51), *Torticola contre Frankensberg* (52), *Pantomimes* (54), *Django Reinhardt* (58). Features: *Pantalaskas, Portrait-robot.* Both were commercial failures and Paviot was unable to continue in the feature film field.

310 PÉRINAL, Georges (1897 – 1965). B: Paris. D: London. Director of photography, with a worldwide reputation. 1913: camera assistant. 1921: became dir. of phot. 1933: England. 1957: U.S.A.

Main films: *Les nouveaux Messieurs, Le Sang d'un poète, David Golder, Gardiens de phare, Sous les toits de Paris, Jean de la lune, Le Million, A nous la liberté, Quatorze Juillet.* Main films abroad: *The Private Life of Henry VIII* (Korda, Britain, 33), *The Private Life of Don Juan* (Korda, Britain, 34), *Things to Come* (Menzies, Britain, 36), *The Thief of Bagdad* (Powell, Britain, 40), *The Fallen Idol* (Reed, Britain, 48), *A King in New York* (Chaplin, Britain, 56), *Bonjour Tristesse* (Preminger, U.S.A., 57), *Oscar Wilde* (Ratoff, Britain, 59).

311 PHILIPE, Gérard (1922 – 1959). B: Cannes. D: Paris. Probably the most famous of all French actors. His outstanding talent and tragically short career have made him a much adored, almost legendary figure. As impressive on stage as he was in films.

Main films: *L'Idiot, Le Diable au corps, La Chartreuse de Parme, Une si jolie petite plage, La Beauté du diable, La Ronde* (50), *Souvenirs perdus, Juliette ou la Clé des songes, Fanfan la Tulipe, Belles de nuit, Les Orgueilleux, Monsieur Ripois, Le Rouge et le noir, Les grandes manœuvres, La meilleure part, Montparnasse 19, Pot-Bouille, Le Joueur, Les Liaisons dangereuses, La Fièvre monte à El Pao.* Directed and acted in *Les Aventures de Till l'Espiègle.*

312 PICCOLI, Michel (1925–). B: Paris. Stage and screen actor. His casual elegance and sensitivity have made him a favourite among leading directors.

Main films: *Le Point du jour, French Cancan, La Mort en ce jardin, Les Sorcières de Salem, Le Doulos, Le Jour et l'heure, Climats, Le Mépris, De l'amour, Le Coup de grâce, Compartiment tueurs, Les Créatures, Les Demoi-selles de Rochefort, Un Homme de trop, La Voleuse, La Guerre est finie; Mon Amour, mon amour; Belle de jour, Benjamin, La Chamade, La Voie lactée, Dillinger e' morto* (Ferreri, Italy, 68), *Topaz* (Hitchcock, U.S.A., 69), *L'Invitée* (De Seta, Italy, 69), *Les Choses de la vie, Max et les ferrailleurs, La Poudre d'escampette.*

313 PIRÈS, Gérard (1942–). B: Paris. Director. His first films show a highly original, sometimes brilliant style. At first photographer, then worked for TV, notably on the "Dim, Dam, Dom" series. Shorts include *Vie et opinions d'Adrien* (65), *Un Misanthrope* (66), *SWB* (68), *La Fête des mères* (69).

Films: *Erotissimo, Fantasia chez les ploucs.*

314 POLLET, Jean-Daniel (1936–). B: Paris. Director. At first some naturalistic

Michel Piccoli and Romy Schneider in LES CHOSES DE LA VIE

shorts (*Pourvu qu'on ait l'ivresse*, 57, *Gala*, 61) and a rather lyrical medium-length film, *Méditerranée* (63). His features are all very original.

Films: *La Ligne de mire* (unfinished). *Une Balle au cœur, Tu imagines Robinson; L'Amour c'est gai, l'amour c'est triste; Le Maître du temps*. Note also his *Rue Saint-Denis* episode about the prostitute and her reluctant client in *Paris vu par . . .*

315 PRESLE, Micheline (1922 –   ). B: Paris. RN: Micheline Chassagne. Actress. Very popular in comedy roles, where her wit and vivaciousness sparkle to best effect. Known in U.S.A. as Micheline Prelle.

Main films: *La Comédie du bonheur, La Nuit fantastique, Falbalas, Boule de suif, Le Diable au corps, Les Jeux sont faits, L'Amour d'une femme, Napoléon, Une Fille pour l'été, Blind Date* (Losey, Britain, 59), *Le Baron de l'Ecluse, L'Amant de cinq jours, L'assassino* (Petri, Italy, 61), *Le Diable et les dix commandements, La Religieuse, Le Roi de cœur, Peau d'âne*.

316 PRÉVERT, Jacques (1900 –   ). B: Neuilly. One of the most famous French scriptwriters. Also poet. A friend of the Surrealists, Prévert brought to the cinema

a blend of sentimentality and anarchic comedy, and both these aspects of his talents exerted a strong influence on the *réalisme poétique* school (q.v.), notably in the films of Carné and Renoir (qq.v.).

Main films: *L'Affaire est dans le sac, Ciboulette, Le Crime de M. Lange, Jenny, Une Partie de campagne* (although his script was not in fact used), *Drôle de drame, Quai des brumes, Le Jour se lève, Remorques, Les Visiteurs du soir, Lumière d'été, Adieu Léonard, Les Enfants du paradis, Aubervilliers* (45), *Les Portes de la nuit, L'Arche de Noé, Voyage-surprise, Les Amants de Vérone, Bim le petit âne* (short), *La Bergère et le ramoneur, Notre-Dame de Paris* (56).

317 PRÉVERT, Pierre (1906 –   ). B: Paris. Director of three excellent burlesque comedies, scripted by his brother JACQUES. At first assistant to Cavalcanti and Renoir (qq.v.). Shorts: *Monsieur Cordon* (33), *Le Commissaire est bon enfant* (34, co. dir. Jacques Becker), *Paris mange son pain* (58), *Paris la belle* (59). Several TV films.

Films: *L'Affaire est dans le sac, Adieu Léonard, Voyage-surprise*.

318 PRÉVOST, Françoise (1930 –   ). B: Paris. Stage and a screen actress. Her elegant sophistication and splendid *hauteur* in a number of intellectual roles have assured her a following. At first model.

Main films: *Les Miracles n'ont lieu qu'une fois, Le bel âge, Paris nous appartient, La Morte-saison des amours, La Fille aux yeux d'or, I sequestrati di Altona* (De Sica, Italy, 62), *Il mare* (Patroni Griffi, Italy, 62), *Il processo di Verona* (Lizzani, Italy, 62), *Vacances portugaises, Galia, L'Une et l'autre, Histoires extraordinaires* (*Metzengerstein* episode), *Mont-Dragon*.

319 RAIMU, Jules (1883 – 1946). B: Toulon. D: Neuilly. RN: Jules Muraire. Actor. At first music hall appearances, then to stage (1900–46). Made his screen name with the Pagnol trilogy (*Marius, Fanny, César*); and it was in Pagnol's work that he had his finest roles, bringing superbly to life the typical Marseillais, with all his humour and worldly wisdom. Raimu was the perfect "monstre sacré." Other films include *Les Gaîtés de l'escadron, Un Carnet de bal, Gribouille, L'étrange M. Victor, Faisons un rêve, Les Perles de la couronne, La Femme du boulanger, Untel père et fils, La Fille du puisatier, L'Arlésienne, L'Homme au chapeau rond.*

320 RAPPENEAU, Jean-Paul (1932–). Fairly important *Nouvelle Vague* scriptwriter, and a regular collaborator of Louis Malle's (q.v.) for several years.

Films (as scriptwriter): *Zazie dans le métro, Vie privée, L'Homme de Rio.* Dialogue only: *Le Combat dans l'île.* As director: *La Vie de château, Les Mariés de l'An Deux.*

Michel Simon and Jean Gabin in QUAI DES BRUMES

321 "RÉALISME POÉTIQUE." Term traditionally assigned to the French film school of the mid and late Thirties because its authentic and meticulous description of social milieux (hence the "realism") was pervaded by romantic and poetic elements deriving from the mythology of Love, Destiny, and the confrontation of Good and Evil, a mythology particularly prominent in the scripts of Jacques Prévert (q.v.).

The most typical products of *réalisme poétique* include the films of Carné, and above all *Quai des brumes* and *Le Jour se lève* (both scripted by Prévert), *Le Crime de M. Lange* (on which Prévert worked) and *Une Partie de campagne* by Renoir, *Remorques* and *Lumière d'été* by Grémillon (with Prévert), *Le grand jeu* and *Pension Mimosas* by Feyder (written by Charles Spaak), *La belle équipe* (written by Spaak) and *Pépé le Moko* by Duvivier.

322 REGGIANI, Serge (1922 –). B: Reggio Emilia. Excellent actor, who has used his almost tragic temperament to full advantage in the various "doomed" or wayward roles he has played. Now also singer.

Main films: *Etoile sans lumière, Les Portes de la nuit, Manon, Les Amants de Vérone, La Ronde* (50), *Secret People* (Dickinson, Britain, 51), *Paris Blues* (Ritt, U.S.A., 61), *Le Doulos, Il gattopardo* (Visconti, Italy, 63), *Compartiment tueurs, Les Aventuriers, L'Armée des ombres, Comptes à rebours.*

323 REICHENBACH, François (1924 –). B: Paris. Director. A driving force in the *cinéma-vérité* (q.v.) movement. Began as a highly original short film-maker. Shorts include *Impressions de New-York* (55), *Houston Texas* (56), *Les Marines* (57). Medium-length social documentary: *La Douceur du village* (64).

Features: *L'Amérique insolite, Un Cœur gros comme ça, Les Amoureux du France* (co.-dir. Pierre Grimblat), *Treize jours en France* (co.-dir. Claude Lelouch), *L'Indiscret; Arthur Rubinstein, l'amour de la vie* (for which he won an Academy Award), *La Caravane d'amour.*

324 RENAUD, Madeleine (1903 –). B: Paris. Actress, mainly on stage (1921 – 46: Comédie-Française; then the theatre company founded by her and her husband, Jean-Louis Barrault, q.v.).

Main films: *Jean de la lune, La Maternelle, L'étrange M. Victor, Remorques, Lumière d'été, Le Ciel est à vous, Le Plaisir, Le Dialogue des Carmélites, Le Diable par la queue.*

325 RENOIR, Claude (1913 –). B: Paris. Nephew of Jean Renoir. Well-known director of photography, one of the finest colour specialists. 1935: becomes dir. of phot.

Main films: *Toni, Une Partie de campagne, Monsieur Vincent, Rendez-vous de Juillet, The River, Le Carrosse d'or, Eléna et les hommes, Les Sorcières de Salem, Une Vie, Les Tricheurs, Et mourir de plaisir, Terrain vague, L'Insoumis, Symphonie pour un massacre, La Curée, Histoires extraordinaires* (*Metzengerstein* episode), *La grande vadrouille, Barbarella, Les Mariés de l'An Deux, Le Casse.*

326 RENOIR, Jean (1894 –). B: Paris. Director. Son of the painter Auguste Renoir, from whom he inherited his *impressionist* (q.v.) talent. The greatest French film-maker, with his best period probably stretching from 1932 to 1939, when he worked in the style of *réalisme poétique* (q.v.). 1940 – 49: U.S.A. Also playwright, novelist, and stage producer. 1960: also TV producer. Acted in *La petite Lili, Le petit chaperon rouge, Une Partie de campagne, La Règle du jeu.*

Films: *La Fille de l'eau, Nana, Charleston, Marquita, La petite marchande d'allumettes, Tire-au-flanc, Le Tournoi, Le Bled, On purge bébé, La Chienne, La Nuit du carrefour, Boudu sauvé des eaux, Chotard et Cie, Madame Bovary, Toni, Le Crime de M. Lange, La Vie*

est à nous, Une Partie de campagne, Les Bas-fonds, La grande illusion, La Marseillaise, La Bête humaine, La Règle du jeu, Tosca (in Italy, only a few shots; film credited to Karl Koch, 40). In U.S.A.: Swamp Water, This Land Is Mine, Salute to France, The Southerner, The Diary of a Chambermaid, The Woman on the Beach. In India: The River. In Italy: Le Carrosse d'or. In France: French Cancan, Eléna et les hommes, Le Déjeuner sur l'herbe, Le Testament du Docteur Cordelier (for TV).

In Austria: Le Caporal épinglé. In France: Le petit théâtre de Jean Renoir.

327 RENOIR, Pierre (1885–1952). B. and D: Paris. Brother of Jean Renoir. Stage and screen actor, usually in supporting parts. From 1928: worked with Louis Jouvet's Theatre Company.

Main films: La Nuit du carrefour, Madame Bovary, La Bandera, La Marseillaise, Les Enfants du paradis.

Opposite: Renoir. Below: Renoir's TONI (courtesy of the Cinémathèque Française)

328 RESNAIS, Alain (1922 –). B: Vannes. The most important director of the *Nouvelle Vague*, preoccupied with the whims and resources of memory. At first stage actor, then an outstanding short film specialist. He did attend IDHEC (q.v.) briefly, but left before his course was completed. Shorts: *Van Gogh* (48), *Guernica* (49), *Gauguin* (50), *L'Alcool tue* (50), *Les Statues meurent aussi* (53, co.-dir. Chris Marker), *Nuit et brouillard* (55), *Toute la mémoire du monde* (56), *Le Mystère de l'atelier 15* (57, co.-dir. Heinrich and Marker), *Le Chant du styrène* (57) etc. Edited *Aux frontières de l'homme, Broadway by Night, La Pointe courte* etc.

At left: Alain Resnais. Below: Claude Rich and Olga Georges-Picot in Resnais's
JE T'AIME, JE T'AIME

Emmanuelle Riva in THÉRÈSE DESQUEYROUX

Features: *Hiroshima mon amour, L'Année dernière à Marienbad, Muriel ou le temps d'un retour, La Guerre est finie, Loin du Vietnam* (one episode); *Je t'aime, je t'aime; Délivrez-nous du bien* (U.S.A./Britain).

329 REYNAUD, Émile (1884 – 1918). B: Montreuil. D: Ivry-sur-Seine. Inventor and director. One of the cinema's leading pioneers. Created the praxinoscope, which enabled him to develop his "théâtre optique" with which he projected his own hand-drawn films (1889), but which was made obsolete by the *Cinématographe*. He is the real inventor of animation (*Un bon bock, Pauvre Pierrot, Autour d'une cabine* etc.).

330 RICH, Claude (1929 –   ). B: Orgeval. Stage and screen actor, much liked for his non-

chalant style and quiet good humour.

Main films: *Les grandes manœuvres, Ce Soir ou jamais, Tout l'or du monde, Les sept péchés capitaux* (*L'Avarice* episode), *Le Caporal épinglé, Les Tontons flingueurs, Les Copains; Mata Hari, agent H 21; L'Or du duc; Mona, l'étoile sans nom; La Mariée était en noir; Je t'aime, je t'aime; Une Veuve en or.*

331 RIVA, Emmanuelle (Emmanuèle) (1927 –   ). B: Chéniménil (Vosges). Actress, at first on stage and then in films. Her overnight success in *Hiroshima mon amour* established her as a mature and extremely photogenic actress.

Main films: *Hiroshima mon amour, Le huitième jour, Recours en grâce, Adua e le compagni* (Bolognini, Italy, 60), *Kapo* (Pontecorvo, Italy, 60); *Léon Morin, prêtre; Climats,*

Thérèse Desqueyroux, Le Coup de grâce, Le gros coup, Thomas l'imposteur, Soledad, Les Risques du métier, L'Homme de désir, La Modification.

332 RIVETTE, Jacques (1928 –). B: Rouen. Director. At first assistant, then shorts: *Bérénice* (50), *Le Quadrille* (50), *Le Divertissement* (52), *Une Visite* (55), *Le Coup du berger* (56). A reticent but profoundly original and thoughtful *auteur*; a key figure in the *Nouvelle Vague*. 1963 – 65: Editor-in-chief of *Cahiers du Cinéma*.

Films: *Paris nous appartient, La Religieuse, L'Amour fou, Out One.*

333 ROBBE-GRILLET, Alain (1922 –). B: Brest. Novelist of the *Nouveau Roman*

school who has turned to cinema in recent years. His visual style is immaculate and he takes an obvious delight in showing how images can give a false impression of the truth. Made his name in films by scripting *L'Année dernière à Marienbad*.

Films: *L'Immortelle, Trans-Europ-Express, L'Homme qui ment, L'Eden et après.*

334 ROBERT, Yves (1920 –). B: Saumur. Actor and director. His comedy performances are deft and intelligent.

Main films (as actor): *Juliette ou la Clé des songes, Les grandes manœuvres, Les mauvaises rencontres, La Jument verte, Le Cinéma de papa.* Main films as director: *Signé Arsène Lupin, La Guerre des boutons, Bébert et*

Jean-Pierre Kalfon and Bulle Ogier in Jacques Rivette's L'AMOUR FOU

Marie-France Pisier and Jean-Louis Trintignant in Alain Robbe Grillet's
TRANS-EUROP-EXPRESS

l'omnibus, Les Copains, Monnaie de singe,
Alexandre le bienheureux, Clérambard.

335 ROBINSON, Madeleine (1916 –
). B: Paris. RN: Madeleine Svoboda.
Stage and screen actress, usually playing
intensely dramatic and romantic parts. Since
1933: theatre. Since 1934: cinema.

Main films: *Lumière d'été, Douce, Sortilèges,*
Les Frères Bouquinquant, Une si jolie petite
plage, Dieu a besoin des hommes, Le Garçon
sauvage, L'Affaire Maurizius, A double tour,
Les Arrivistes, Léviathan, Le Procès (Welles,
62), *Piège pour Cendrillon, Le petit matin.*

336 ROHMER, Eric (1920 –). B:
Nancy. Critic and director. Since 1945: critic

and theorist, at first using his real name
Maurice Schérer. 1957 – 63: joint Editor-in-
chief of *Cahiers du Cinéma.* Has scripted all his
own films and Godard's *Tous les garçons*
s'appellent Patrick. Also TV work. His features are part of a series entitled *contes moraux*
and show his keen interest in moral and psychological analysis. Shorts and medium-length
features: *Présentation ou Charlotte et son steak*
(51), *Bérénice* (54), *La Sonate à Kreutzer* (56),
La Boulangère de Monceau (62), *La Carrière*
de Suzanne (63), *Nadja à Paris* (64) etc.

Films: *Le Signe du Lion, Paris vu par . . .*
(*Place de l'Etoile* episode), *La Collectionneuse,*
Ma Nuit chez Maud, Le Genou de Claire.

337 ROMANCE, Viviane (1912 –). B:
Roubaix. RN: Pauline Ortmans. Actress.

1930: "Miss Paris." Then music hall. Became the number one "vamp" of the Thirties with her sexy charm.

Main films: *Ciboulette, La Bandéra, Pépé le Moko, La belle équipe, Le Puritain, Naples au baiser de feu, Prison de femmes, L'étrange M. Victor, La Maison du Maltais, La Vénus aveugle, Carmen, Panique, Tournant dangereux, Mélodie en sous-sol.*

338 RONET, Maurice (1927–). B: Nice. Actor, with an ironic and elegant style. Studied drama at the Conservatoire.

Main films: *Rendez-vous de Juillet, La jeune folle, Châteaux en Espagne, Les Aristocrates, Celui qui doit mourir, Ascenseur pour l'échafaud, Plein soleil, Le Rendez-vous de minuit, Portrait-robot, La Dénonciation, The Victors* (Foreman,

Britain, 63), *La Ronde* (64), *Trois chambres à Manhattan, La longue marche, La Ligne de démarcation, Le Scandale, La Route de Corinthe, Les Oiseaux vont mourir au Pérou, La Femme infidèle, La Piscine, La Femme écarlate, Les Femmes, Le dernier saut; Un peu, beaucoup passionnément; La Modification, Qui?, Raphaël ou le débauché.* Directed and acted in *Le Voleur du Tibidabo.*

339 ROSAY, Françoise (1891–). B: Paris. RN: Françoise de Nalèche. Stage actress (*début* at Odéon in 1908) and then, from 1913, in films, especially those directed by her husband Jacques Feyder* (q.v.). Always plays rather grand ladies with authority and wit.

Main films: *Crainquebille*, Gribiche*, Le grand jeu*, Pension Mimosas*, La Kermesse*

Opposite: Françoise Rosay in FAUT PAS PRENDRE LES ENFANTS DU BON DIEU POUR DES CANARDS SAUVAGES. Below: Maurice Ronet (centre), Hubert Deschamps and Jacques Sereys in LE FEU FOLLET

héroïque*, Jenny, Un Carnet de bal, Drôle de drame, Les Gens du voyage*, La Symphonie des brigands (Friedrich Feher, Britain, 38), *L'Auberge rouge, Le Joueur, Le Bois des amants, La métamorphose des cloportes, Faut pas prendre les enfants du bon dieu pour des canards sauvages.*

340 ROSSIF, Frédéric (1922 –). B: Cetinje, Montenegro. TV director (several programmes, mostly documentaries), and also a specialist in compilation films for the cinema, drawing intelligently on the resources of old newsreels and archive materials.

Films: *Le Temps du ghetto, Mourir à Madrid, Les Animaux* (also scripted), *Révolution d'Octobre, Un Mur à Jerusalem* (co.-dir. Albert Knobler), *Pourquoi l'Amérique, Aussi loin que l'amour.*

341 ROUCH, Jean (1917 –). B: Paris. Director of ethnographical films. At first

engineer. He has used 16 mm film as a means of making sociological documentaries on Black Africa; all his work has an extraordinarily humane appeal. One of the major figures of *cinéma-vérité.*

Main films (shorts): *Initiation à la danse des possédés* (48), *La Circoncision* (48), *Bataille sur le grand fleuve* (50), *Les fils de l'eau* (55), *Les Maîtres fous* (56), *Monsieur Albert prophète* (60). Features: *Moi un Noir, La Pyramide humaine, Chronique d'un été* (co.-dir. Edgar Morin), *La Punition, Paris vu par . . . (Gare du Nord* episode), *La Chasse au lion à l'arc, Jaguar, Petit à petit.*

342 ROUFFIO, Jacques (1928 –). Director. Assistant and technical adviser for several years.

Film: *L'Horizon.*

343 ROULEAU, Raymond (1904 –). B: Brussels. Stage and screen actor, and an attractive star of the Forties.

Main films (as actor): *L'Assassinat du Père Noël, Dernier atout, Falbalas.* As director: *Le Couple idéal* (co.-dir. Bernard Roland), *Les Sorcières de Salem, Les Amants de Teruel.*

344 ROULLET, Serge (1926 –). B: Bordeaux. Director. At first assistant to Hans Richter in New York, then to Bresson. Also short film-maker: *Viennent les jours* (60), *Sillages* (64).

Films: *Le Mur, Benito Cereno.* Technical adviser on *Jupiter.*

345 ROUQUIER, Georges (1909 –) B: Lunel-Viel. Director. At first worked as linotype operator; then shorts, all remarkably simple, observant, and direct: *Vendanges* (29) *Le Tonnelier* (42), *Le Charron* (43), *Le Chaudronnier* (49), *Le Sel de la terre* (50), *Malgover* (52), *Arthur Honegger* (55) etc.

Films: *Farrebique, Sang et lumière, Lourdes et ses miracles* (doc.), *SOS Noronha.*

Michel Piccoli and Romy Schneider in LES CHOSES DE LA VIE

346 ROZIER, Jacques (1926–). B: Paris. Director. At first IDHEC (q.v.). Then shorts: *Rentrée des classes* (53), *Blue jeans* (58), *Les Paparazzi* (64) etc. Also TV series work.

Films: *Adieu Philippine* (a masterpiece of romantic cinema), *Chichifrichi.*

347 RUSPOLI, Mario (1925–). B: Rome. Writer, then documentarist (see *cinéma-vérité*): *Les Hommes de la baleine* (56), *Ombre et lumière de Rome* (56), *Les Inconnus de la terre* (62), *Regards sur la folie* (62), *Renaissance* (in Tunisia, 66). Since 1967: TV work.

348 SADOUL, Georges (1904–1967). B: Nancy. D: Paris. Film historian who before his death had achieved a worldwide reputation. He was the first writer to study cinema history in terms of economics, politics, and techniques. He had an enormous collection of material and put it to good use in his various reference books. Sadoul was also a leading light of the now-famous "Critics' Week" at the Cannes Festival.

Main publications: "Histoire générale du cinéma" (48–54, unfinished), "Histoire du cinéma mondial" (49), "Les Merveilles du cinéma" (57), "Vie de Charlot" (57), "Georges Méliès" (61), "Dictionnaire des films" (65), "Dictionnaire des cinéastes" (65), "Gérard Philipe" (67).

349 SAULNIER, Jacques (1928–). B: Paris. Well-known set designer. At first assistant to Douy and Trauner (qq.v.). Began his own work in collaboration with Bernard Evein (q.v.).

Main films (alone): *L'Année dernière à Marienbad, La Morte-saison des amours, La Proie pour l'ombre, Education sentimentale, L'Aîné des Ferchaux, Landru, Muriel, Du Mouron pour les petits oiseaux, La Guerre est finie, La Vie de château, La Prisonnière, Ho!, Le Clan des Siciliens, Le Chat, Le Casse.*

350 SAUTET, Claude (1924–). B: Montrouge. Director. 1948: IDHEC (q.v.). At first assistant, TV producer, and scriptwriter (*Peau de banane, Symphonie pour un massacre, La Vie de château, La Mise à sac, La Chamade,*

Le Diable par la queue, Borsalino). An interesting figure, somewhat on the edge of the *Nouvelle Vague.*

Films: *Bonjour sourire, Classe tous risques, L'Arme à gauche, Les Choses de la vie, Max et les ferrailleurs.*

351 SCHOENDOERFFER, Pierre (1928–). B: Chamaillières. Director. At first news photographer. After three mediocre films, he suddenly took a great step forward with his picture of men at war, *La 317ème section,* and in 1969 became a best-selling novelist.

Films: *La Passe du diable, Ramuntcho, Pêcheur d'Islande, La 317ème section* (also script), *Objectif 500 millions* (also script), *La Patrouille Anderson* (for TV, Academy Award), *Le Désert des Tartares.*

352 SCHROEDER, Barbet (1941–). B: Teheran. Director. At first critic (1958–63) and producer ("Les Films du Losange"). Began his directing career with the con-troversial and respected *More.*

Films (as producer): *Paris vu par . . .* (also acted), *La Collectionneuse, Tu imagines Robinson, Ma Nuit chez Maud.*

353 SCHUFTAN, Eugène (1893–). B: Wroclaw/Breslau. RN: Eugen Schüfftan. German director of photography. Spent most of his career in France and the U.S.A. An international reputation, especially during the Thirties. Pioneered the "Schüfftan Process," first used in *Metropolis.*

Main films: *Menschen am Sonntag* (Siodmak/Wilder, Germany, 29), *L'Atlantide* (Pabst, France, 31), *La tendre ennemie, Mademoiselle Docteur* (Pabst, France, 37), *Drôle de drame, Quai des brumes, La Symphonie des brigands* (Friedrich Feher, Britain, 38), *C'est arrivé demain, Le Rideau cramoisi, Mina de Vanghel, Marianne de ma jeunesse, La Tête contre les murs, Les Yeux sans visage, Un Couple, The Hustler* (Rossen, U.S.A., 61), *Les Vierges, Lilith* (Rossen, U.S.A., 63), *Trois chambres à Manhattan.*

354 SÉCHAN, Edmond (1919–). B: Montpellier. Director of photography (and director). Several shorts as lighting cameraman (including *Crin blanc*) and some features, including *Le Ballon rouge* (medium-length), *Le Monde du silence, Mort en fraude, Les Dragueurs, L'Homme de Rio, Le Ciel sur la tête, Les Tribulations d'un Chinois en Chine, Tendre voyou, A cœur joie, La Peau de torpédo, Le lis de mer, Sur un arbre perché.* Directed shorts, among them *Niok le petit éléphant, Histoire d'un poisson rouge,* and features: *L'Ours, Pour un amour lointain.*

355 SERVAIS, Jean (1910–). B: Antwerp. Actor. Began in the theatre, then turned to cinema (from 1931) as a handsome young lead. After the war he played many major romantic roles, all marked by his tight-

Pierre Schoendoerffer's LA 317ème SECTION

lipped, rather melancholy personality.

Main films: *Angèle, La Danse de mort, Une si jolie petite plage, Le Château de verre, Le Plaisir, Rue de l'Estrapade, Mina de Vanghel, Du Rififi chez les hommes* (Dassin, France, 54), *Celui qui doit mourir* (Dassin, France, 56), *La Fièvre monte à El Pao, L'Homme de Rio, Thomas l'Imposteur, Seduto alla sua destra* (Zurlini, Italy, 68).

356 SEYRIG, Delphine (1932 –). B: Beirut. Actress. At first stage work in New York (where she took part in Robert Frank's *Pull My Daisy*). Her very real ability and the serene, almost hypnotic quality of her looks were first revealed by Resnais (q.v.). Also TV work. Her brother, Francis Seyrig, wrote the organ music for *L'Année dernière à Marienbad*, and the score for *Marie Soleil*.

Films: *Pull My Daisy, L'Année dernière à Marienbad, Muriel, La Musica, Mr. Freedom, Baisers volés, La Voie lactée, Peau d'âne.*

357 SIGNORET, Simone (1921 –). B: Wiesbaden. RN: Simone Kaminker. Actress of considerable talent and sensual appeal, often playing self-confident but troubled women.

Main films: *Macadam, Dédée d'Anvers, Manèges, La Ronde* (50), *Casque d'or, Thérèse Raquin, Les Diaboliques, La Mort en ce jardin, Les Sorcières de Salem, Room at the Top*

Opposite: Delphine Seyrig in L'ANNÉE DERNIÈRE À MARIENBAD. Below: Simone Signoret in L'AVEU

(Clayton, Britain, 58), *Les mauvais coups, Le Jour et l'heure, Term of Trial* (Glenville, Britain, 62), *Dragées au poivre, Ship of Fools* (Kramer, U.S.A., 65), *Compartiment tueurs, Paris brûle-t-il?, The Deadly Affair* (Lumet, Britain, 67), *The Sea Gull* (Lumet, Britain, 68), *L'Armée des ombres, L'Aveu, L'Américain, Le Chat, Comptes à rebours.*

358 SIGURD, Jacques (1920 –). B: Paris. Scriptwriter. At first actor and journalist. An important writer in the naturalist period after the war (1945 – 55).

Main films: *Dédée d'Anvers, Une si jolie petite plage, Manèges, Les Miracles n'ont lieu qu'une fois, La jeune folle, L'Air de Paris, La meilleure part, Les Tricheurs, Du Mouron pour les petits oiseaux, Trois chambres à Manhattan.*

359 SIMON, Jean-Daniel (1942 –). Director. A promising member of the latest generation in French cinema.

Films: *La Fille d'en face* (scripted by Polanski), *Adélaïde, Ils.*

360 SIMON, Michel (1895 –). B: Geneva. Major stage and screen actor; an

authentic "monstre sacré" with his blend of vitality, truculence, and sly wit. From 1911: boxer and music hall acrobat. Since 1920: theatre work.

Main films: *Feu Mathias Pascal, La Passion de Jeanne d'Arc* (Dreyer, France, 28), *Tire-au-flanc* (28), *Jean de la lune, On purge bébé, La Chienne, Boudu sauvé des eaux, L'Atalante, La Mort en fuite, Naples au baiser de feu, Drôle de drame, Les Disparus de Saint-Agil, Quai des brumes, La Fin du jour, Fric-Frac, Les Musiciens du ciel, Boule de suif, Panique, La Beauté du diable, La Poison, La Vie d'un honnête homme, Austerlitz, Candide, Cyrano et d'Artagnan, The Train* (Frankenheimer, U.S.A., 64), *Le vieil homme et l'enfant, La Maison, Blanche.*

361 SIMON, Simone (1914 –). B: Marseille. Stage and screen actress. Delicate and graceful feminine lead in the Thirties.

Main films: *Lac aux dames, La Bête humaine, Olivia, La Ronde* (50), *Le Plaisir.* Her career in the U.S.A. (1936 – 46) was disappointing, save for her extraordinary triumph in *Cat People* (Jacques Tourneur, 42).

362 SIMONIN, Albert (1905 –). B: Paris. Thriller writer with an ear for local slang, using it in his scripts, adaptations, and dialogue.

Main films: *Touchez pas au grisbi, Des Femmes disparaissent, Une Balle dans le canon, Du Mouron pour les petits oiseaux, Le Gentleman d'Epsom, Mélodie en sous-sol, La Métamorphose des cloportes, Tendre voyou.*

363 SOLOGNE, Madeleine (1912 –). B: La Ferte Imbault. Stage and screen actress. A romantic, sylph-like star of the Forties.

Main films: *Les Gens du voyage, L'éternel retour, La Foire aux chimères, Une grande fille toute simple.*

Opposite: Michel Simon and Séverine Lerczinska in BOUDU SAUVÉ DES EAUX

364 SPAAK, Charles (1903–). B: Brussels. Highly respected scriptwriter, who contributed in no small way to the success of both Renoir and Feyder (qq.v.). Belgian-born, but worked in France from 1928 onwards.

Main films: *Les nouveaux Messieurs, La petite Lise, Le grand jeu, Pension Mimosas, La Kermesse héroïque, La Bandera, Les Bas-fonds, La belle équipe, Gueule d'amour, La grande illusion, La Fin du jour, L'étrange M. Victor, Untel père et fils, L'Assassinat du Père Noël, Le Ciel est à vous, L'Idiot, Panique, Justice est faite, La Nuit est mon royaume, Nous sommes tous des assassins, Avant le déluge, Thérèse Raquin, Le Dossier noir, Cartouche, Germinal.*

365 STAREWITCH, Ladislas (1892– 1965). B: Moscow. D: Paris. Animator, who spent his youth running a Natural History Museum in Russia and moved to France in 1921. As early as 1911 in Moscow he was making animal puppet films. In France he was responsible for several similar productions, all rich in charm and fantasy: *La Nuit de Noël* (11), *Rousslan et Ludmilla* (11), *Le Noël des habitants de la forêt* (12), *La Voix du Rossignol* (22), *La Cigale et la fourmi* (24), *L'Horloge magique* (25), *Zanzabelle à Paris* (49). Feature: *Le Roman de Renart* (1928–39).

366 STROHEIM, Erich von (1885–1957). D: Maurepas. Actor and director who worked and lived for some time in France, where he died. All his roles had a magnificent power and distinction.

Main films (as actor in France): *La grande illusion, Mademoiselle Docteur, Alibi, Les Pirates du rail, Les Disparus de Saint-Agil, Macao l'enfer du jeu, Menaces, La Danse de mort* (also scripted), *Napoléon* (54).

367 SYLVIE (1885–1970). B: Paris. RN: Thérèse Sylvie. Stage and screen actress from 1912 onwards. Played the stern and authorita-

tive lady with only modest success until her astonishing "come-back" in *La vieille dame indigne*.

Main films: *Un Carnet de bal, Le Corbeau, Les Anges du péché, L'Idiot, Le Diable au corps, Pattes blanches, Thérèse Raquin, Le Dossier noir, Le Miroir à deux faces, Château en Suède, La vieille dame indigne, J'ai tué Raspoutine.*

368 TATI, Jacques (1908–). B: Le Pecq, Seine-et-Oise. Actor and director. Began as music hall comedian. Then appeared in, and wrote, a number of shorts: *Oscar champion de tennis* (also dir., 32), *On demande une brute* (34), *Gai dimanche* (35), *Soigne ton gauche* (36), *L'Ecole des facteurs* (also dir., 37), *Retour à*

Opposite: Jacques Tati in PLAYTIME

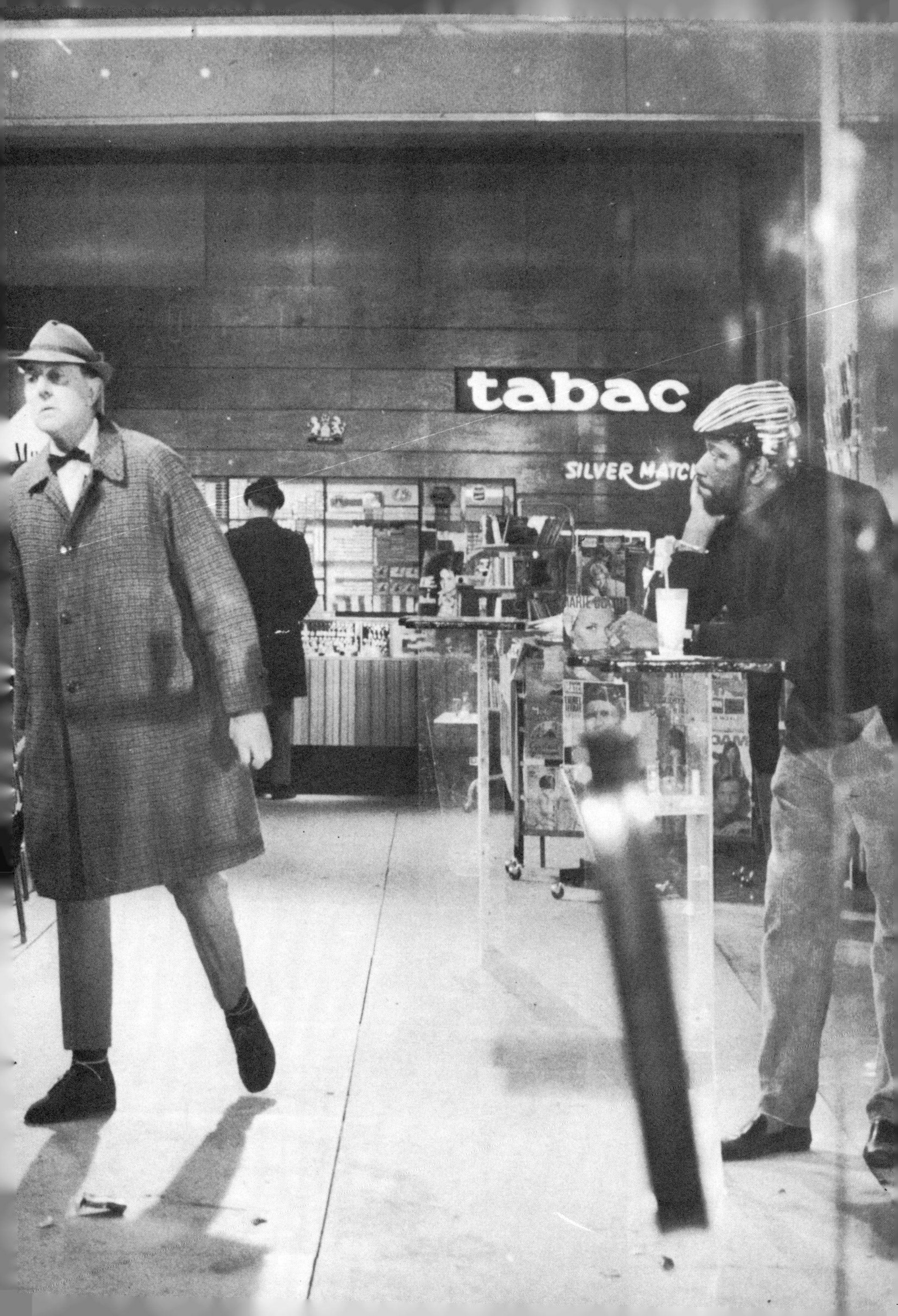
tabac

la terre (also dir., 45). Also acted (bit part) in *Sylvie et le fantôme* and *Le Diable au corps*. Tati is one of the most original comedians in the French cinema and in a comparatively sparse output he has created a universe entirely his own.

Films (as director, writer, and actor): *Jour de fête, Les Vacances de M. Hulot, Mon Oncle, Playtime, Trafic.*

369 T E R Z I E F F, Laurent (1935 –   ). B: Paris. RN: Laurent Tchemerzine. Stage and screen actor of the *Nouvelle Vague* generation, usually playing romantic roles.

Main films: *Les Tricheurs, Kapo* (Ponte-corvo, Italy, 60), *Les Régates de San Francisco, Le Bois des amants, Vanina Vanini* (Rossellini, Italy, 61), *Ballade pour un voyou, Soledad, A cœur joie, La Prisonnière, La Voie lactée.*

370 T H I R A R D, Armand (1899 –   ). B: Nantes. Director of photography since 1928; has worked with the leading French directors. Admired for the classical quality of his work and for his adroit use of colour.

Main films: *David Golder, Poil de carotte, La Tête d'un homme, Gribouille, Hôtel du Nord, Remorques, Fric-Frac, L'Assassinat du Père*

Jacques Tati in MON ONCLE

Laurent Terzieff in KAPO

Noël, *La Symphonie fantastique, La Symphonie pastorale, Le Silence est d'or, Quai des Orfèvres, Manon, Le Salaire de la peur, Belles de nuit, Les Diaboliques, Et Dieu créa la femme, Sait-on jamais, Les Bijoutiers du clair de lune, Babette s'en va-t-en guerre, Les Régates de San Francisco, La Vérité, Le Repos du guerrier, Château en Suède, Piège pour Cendrillon, Le Cerveau.*

371 THIRIET, Maurice (1906–). B: Meulan. Composer, pupil of Maurice Jaubert (q.v.). Worked for the cinema since 1933.

Main film scores: *La Nuit fantastique, Les visiteurs du soir, Les Enfants du paradis,*

L'Idiot, Une si jolie petite plage, Fanfan la Tulipe, Thérèse Raquin, L'Air de Paris, Crime et châtiment, Les grandes familles, Les Yeux de l'amour.

372 TISSIER, Jean (1896–). B: Paris. Comedy actor who has featured in many films, most of them mediocre.

Main films: *Battements de cœur, Nous les gosses, Premier rendez-vous, Le dernier des six, Les Inconnus dans la maison, L'Assassin habite au 21, Gigi, Si Versailles m'était conté; Papa, maman, la bonne et moi; Papa, maman, ma femme et moi; Si Paris nous était conté, Candide,*

127

Les Godelureaux; Vive Henri IV, vive l'amour; La Bride sur le cou, Snobs, Les Vierges, L'Or du duc.

373 TRAUNER, Alexandre (1906–). B: Budapest. Set designer, assistant to Lazare Meerson (q.v.) until 1935. Respected for the naturalism of his sets, especially in Carné's* films. Since 1960 he has been involved primarily with American productions in Europe and the U.S.A.

Main films: *L'Affaire est dans le sac, Drôle de drame*, Quai des brumes*, Entrée des artistes, Le Jour se lève*, Remorques, Lumière d'été, Les Visiteurs du soir* (co. Georges Wakhevitch), Les Enfants du paradis*, Les Portes de la nuit*,*

Voyage surprise, Manèges, La Marie du port, Juliette ou la Clé des songes*, Les Miracles n'ont lieu qu'une fois, Othello* (Welles, 50), *Les Mariés de l'An Deux.*

374 TRINTIGNANT, Jean-Louis (1930–). B: Pont Saint-Esprit, Nîmes. Actor of the *Nouvelle Vague* generation. His career really began after a short spell in the theatre, when Vadim (q.v.) starred him opposite Brigitte Bardot (q.v.) in *Et Dieu créa la femme.* His shy humour, intelligence, and discretion have helped him to maintain his prominent position in French cinema. Also TV work.

Main films: *Si tous les gars du monde, Et Dieu créa la femme, Les Liaisons dangereuses,*

Jean-Louis Trintignant in MATA-HARI, AGENT H-21

Above: Valerie Legrange and Jean-Louis Trintignant in Nadine Trintignant's MON AMOUR, MON AMOUR. Below: François Truffaut

Austerlitz, Pleins feux sur l'assassin, Le Cœur battant, Parfois le dimanche (short, Ado Kyrou), *Le Combat dans l'île, Le Jeu de la vérité, Il sorpasso* (Risi, Italy, 62), *Château en Suède; Mata Hari, agent H 21; Compartiment tueurs, Le dix-septième ciel, Le longue marche, Paris brûle-t-il?, Un Homme et une femme, Trans-Europ-Express; Mon Amour, mon amour; L'Homme qui ment, Les Biches, Z, Le Voleur des crimes, Metti una sera a cena* (Patroni Griffi, Italy, 69), *Ma Nuit chez Maud, Il conformista* (Bertolucci, Italy, 70), *L'Américain, Le Voyou, L'Homme au cerveau greffé.*

375 TRINTIGNANT, Nadine (1934 –   ). B: Nice. Wife of JEAN-LOUIS Trintignant. At first script girl, editor, short film-maker (*Fragilité, ton nom est femme*, 56).

Films (also scripts): *Mon Amour, mon amour; Le Voleur de crimes, Ça n'arrive qu'aux autres.*

376 TRUFFAUT, François (1932 –   ). B: Paris. Director. One of the finest representa-

tives of the *Nouvelle Vague*. At first critic, well known for his violent attacks on *le cinéma de*

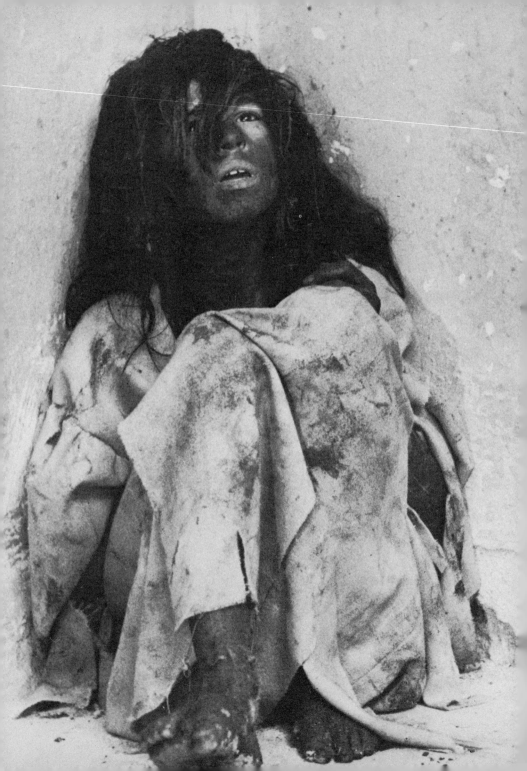

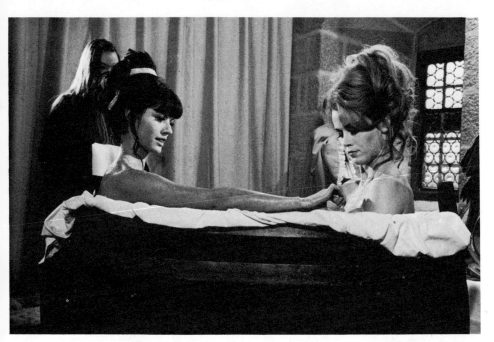

Above: A scene from the Vadim episode of HISTOIRES EXTRAORDINAIRES. Opposite:
Jean-Pierre Cargol in Truffaut's L'ENFANT SAUVAGE. Below: Roger Vadim

papa and his campaign for simplicity and sincerity of approach. At first shorts: *Une Visite* (54), *Les Mistons* (58), *Une Histoire d'eau* (co-dir. Godard). Also co-produced *Le Testament d'Orphée, Paris nous appartient, Tire-au-flanc* (61), *Une grosse tête* and all his own films through his company, "Les Films du Carrosse." Co-scripted *Mata Hari, agent H 21* and all his own films.

Films: *Les 400 coups, Tirez sur le pianiste, Jules et Jim, L'Amour à vingt ans* (one episode), *La Peau douce, Fahrenheit 451* (in Britain), *La Mariée était en noir, Baisers volés, La Sirène du Mississipi, L'Enfant sauvage, Domicile conjugal.*

377 VADIM, Roger (1928 –   ). B: Paris. RN: Roger Vadim Plemiannikov. Director. At first stage actor (1944 – 47), assistant,

journalist, scriptwriter, and TV director. His first film is regarded as one of the pioneer works of the *Nouvelle Vague*; since then, Vadim has opted for a more commercial, superficial approach to cinema. Acted in *Dragées au poivre, Le Testament d'Orphée.* Scripted and prod. *Et Satan conduit le bal.* Scripted *Futures vedettes, Cette sacrée gamine, En effeuillant la marguerite.*

Films (all scripted except*): *Et Dieu créa la femme, Sait-on jamais, Les Bijoutiers du clair de lune, Les Liaisons dangereuses, Et mourir de plaisir, La Bride sur le cou, Les sept péchés capitaux* (one episode), *Le Vice et la vertu, Le Repos du guerrier, Château en Suède, La Ronde* (64)*, *La Curée, Barbarella, Histoires extraordinaires* (*Metzengerstein* episode).

378 VALÈRE, Jean (1925 –   ). B: Paris. Director. At first assistant, then shorts, including *Paris la nuit* (co.-dir. Jacques Baratier, 55).

Charles Vanel and Brigitte Bardot in LA VÉRITÉ

Films: *La Sentence, Les grandes personnes, Le gros coup, La Femme écarlate, Mont-Dragon.*

379 VANEL, Charles (1892 –   ). B: Rennes. Stage and screen actor. A powerful personality who has left his mark on over two hundred films. 1908: stage *début* in Paris. 1912: enters cinema. Also several appearances in Italian films.

Main films: *La Proie du vent, Dainah la Métisse, Les Croix de bois, Le grand jeu, La belle équipe, Jenny, Abus de confiance, Les Pirates du rail, La Loi du Nord, Le Ciel est à vous, Le Salaire de la peur, L'Affaire Maurizius, Si Versailles m'était conté, Les Diaboliques, To Catch a Thief* (Hitchcock, U.S.A., 55), *La Mort en ce jardin, La Vérité, Rififi à Tokyo, L'Aîné des Ferchaux, Symphonie pour un massacre, Le Chant du monde, Les Tribulations d'un Chinois en Chine, Un Homme de trop, Ballade pour un chien, La Nuit bulgare, Ils, Comptes à rebours.*

380 VAN PARYS, Georges (1902–1971). B and D: Paris. Prolific composer; also songs, operettas.

Main film scores: *Le Million, Abus de confiance, Circonstances atténuantes, Premier bal, Marie Martine, Le Silence est d'or, La Vie en rose, Fanfan la Tulipe, Casque d'or, Trois Femmes, Les Belles de Nuit, Madame de . . ., Rue de l'Estrapade* (co.), *Avant le déluge, L'Affaire Maurizius, Les Diaboliques, French Cancan, Les grandes manœuvres, Montparnasse 19, Tout l'or du monde, Les Fêtes galantes.*

381 VARDA, Agnès (1928 –   ). B: Brussels. Woman director. Also stills photographer. Married to Jacques DEMY. Also TV

Antoine Bourseiller and Corinne Marchand in Agnès Varda's CLÉO DE 5 À 7

work. Medium-length film: *La Pointe courte* (54, one of the precursors of the *Nouvelle Vague*). Shorts: *O Saisons, O châteaux* (57), *Du Côté de la côte* (58), *L'Opéra-Mouffe* (58), *La Cocotte d'azur* (59), *Salut les Cubains* (in Cuba, 63), *Oncle Janco* (67), *Black Panthers* (68).

Films: *Cléo de 5 à 7, Le Bonheur, Les Créatures, Loin du Vietnam* (collaboration), *Lions Love* (in U.S.A.).

382 VARÉLA, José (1933 –   ). Director. At first actor, assistant, and shorts. One of the most dynamic directors of the new generation.

Films: *Mamaia, Money Money.*

383 VÉDRÈS, Nicole (1911 – 1965). B. and D: Paris. Woman writer, essayist, director, and a distinguished member of the Parisian intelli-gentsia. Shorts: *Amazone* (51), *Aux frontières de l'homme* (53).

Films: *Paris 1900, La Vie commence demain.*

384 VENTURA, Lino (1919 –   ). B: Parma. RN: Lino Borrini. A powerful, serious actor, specialising in "tough guy" roles. In recent years he has become something of a second Gabin (q.v.).

Main films: *Touchez pas au grisbi, Razzia sur la chnouf, Crime et châtiment* (56), *Ascenseur pour l'échafaud, Maigret tend un piège, Montparnasse 19, Classe tous risques, Un Taxi pour Tobrouk, Les Tontons flingueurs, Cent mille dollars au soleil, L'Arme à gauche, Les grandes gueules, Le deuxième souffle, Les Aventuriers, Le Rapace, Le Clan des Siciliens, L'Armée des ombres, Dernier domicile connu, Boulevard du*

Opposite: Marie-France Boyer and Jean-Claude Drouot in LE BONHEUR. Below: Lino Ventura in DERNIER DOMICILE CONNU

rhum, Fantasia chez les ploucs; Laisse aller, c'est une valse.

385 VERGEZ, Gérard (1935–). Director. At first stage producer. Has written and directed an engaging first feature: *Ballade pour un chien.* Then: *Teresa.*

386 VERNEUIL, Henri (1920–). B: Rhodes. Director, whose work is aimed unashamedly and exclusively at the box-office. At first specialist in short films.

Main films: *La Table aux crevés, Le Fruit défendu, L'Ennemi public no. 1, Le Mouton à cinq pattes, Des gens sans importance, La Vache et le prisonnier, Le Président, Un Singe en hiver, Mélodie en sous-sol, Cent mille dollars au soleil, Week-end à Zuydcoote, The 25th Hour, Guns for San Sebastian, Le Clan des Siciliens, Le Casse.*

387 VERNON, Anne (1925–). B: Saint Denis. Stage and screen actress, usually starred in light comedy roles where her gay personality appears to best effect.

Main films: *Edouard et Caroline, Rue de l'Estrapade, Bel Ami, Arsène Lupin contre Arsène Lupin, Les Parapluies de Cherbourg.*

388 VERSOIS, Odile (1930–). B: Paris. RN: Katiana de Poliakoff-Baïdaroff. A subtle and attractive actress, whose delicate playing has been less appreciated than her sister's (Marina Vlady, q.v.).

Main films: *Dernières vacances, Mina de Vanghel, Check point* (Thomas, Britain, 56), *Toi le venin, Cartouche; A cause, à cause d'une femme; Benjamin.*

389 VÉRY, Pierre (1900–1960). B: Bellon (Charente). Writer and scriptwriter, well known for the suspense and dramatic atmosphere of his thrillers.

Main films: *Les Disparus de Saint-Agil, L'Assassinat du Père Noël, Goupi mains rouges, Le Pays sans étoiles, La Chartreuse de Parme, Souvenirs perdus, Un grand patron.*

390 VIERNY, Sacha (1919–). B: Boisle-Roi. At first assistant and director of a number of shorts. Main shorts as lighting cameraman: *Tu enfanteras sans douleur* (Fabiani, 55), *Le Chant du styrène* (Resnais), *Lettre de Sibérie* (Marker).

Main films: *Le bel âge, Hiroshima mon amour, Merci Natercia, La Morte-saison des amours, L'Année dernière à Marienbad, Climats, Aimez-vous les femmes?, Muriel, La Guerre est finie, La Musica, Belle de jour, Le Tatoué, La Nuit bulgare.*

391 VIGO, Jean (1905–1934). B. and D: Paris. RN: Jean Almereyda. One of the most celebrated of French directors, who died young after a brief but dazzling career. With his unparalleled blend of realism and surrealism, Vigo impressed also by his lyricism, his ironic observation, and his socially and morally anarchic attitude to life.

Films: *A propos de Nice; Taris, champion de natation* (short, 31), *Zéro de conduite, L'Atalante.*

PRIX JEAN VIGO. Founded in 1951 to commemorate the director and awarded annually to a film with social values. Winners during the past twelve years: *Le beau Serge, A bout de souffle, La Peau et les os, La Guerre*

Jean Gabin, Henri Verneuil and Henri Decaë on the set of LE CLAN DES SICILIENS

des boutons, Mourir à Madrid, La Jetée, La belle vie, La Noire de . . . (Sembène, 66), *Qui êtes-vous, Polly Maggoo?; O Salto, L'Enfance nue, Hoa-Binh.*

392 VILAR, Jean (1916–). B: Sète. Actor. Head of the Théâtre National Populaire (1951–63), where he accomplished a great deal in the staging of modern drama. His film appearances have been rare but always striking and offbeat.

Main films: *Les Portes de la nuit, Les Frères Bouquinquant, La Ferme des sept péchés, Les Eaux troubles, Les Aventures de Till l'Espiègle, Des Christ par milliers, Le petit matin, Raphaël ou le débauché.*

393 VILARDEBO, Carlos (1926–). B: Lisbon. Director. At first assistant. Some highly original and outstanding shorts, including *Vivre* (58), *L'Eau et la pierre* (59), *La petite cuiller* (60), *Le Cirque Calder* (61), *Véronique ou les jeunes filles* (63).

Film: *Les Iles enchantées.*

394 VLADY, Marina (1938–). B: Clichy. Blonde actress, with immense poise and grace, having matured from the "bad seed" roles she played as a 'teenager. 1944–49: ballet dancer. Sister of Odile Versois (q.v.).

Main films: *Avant le déluge, Les Salauds vont en enfer, La Sorcière, Pardonnez nos offenses, Crime et châtiment, Toi le venin, La Sentence, La Nuit des espions, La Princesse de Clèves, La ragazza in vetrina* (Emmer, Italy, 60), *Adorable menteuse, Climats, Les sept péchés capitaux, Les bonnes causes, L'ape regina* (Ferreri, Italy, 63), *Dragées au poivre, Le Meurtrier, On*

a volé la Joconde; Mona, pour une étoile sans nom; Chimes at Midnight (Welles, Spain/ Switzerland, 66), *Deux ou trois choses que je sais d'elle, Le Temps de vivre, Subject for a Short Story* (Yutkevich, U.S.S.R., 69), *La Nuit bulgare.*

395 WADEMANT, Annette (1928–). B: Brussels. Scriptwriter. Came to prominence after her collaboration on Becker's early films, to which she brought elegance and verve.

Main films: *Edouard et Caroline, Rue de l'Estrapade, Madame de . . ., Lola Montès, Typhon sur Nagasaki, Une Parisienne, Faibles femmes, Comment réussir en amour, La Leçon particulière.*

396 WAKHÉVITCH, Georges (1907–). B: Odessa. Set and costume designer. A

Dita Parlo and Michel Simon in Jean Vigo's L'ATALANTE

considerable body of work in both theatre (from 1927) and cinema. Also painter. Assistant to Lazare Meerson (q.v.).

Main films: *L'Homme à l'Hispano, La Tête d'un homme, Madame Bovary, La grande illusion, La Marseillaise, La Maison du Maltais, Les Visiteurs du soir* (co. Trauner; also costumes), *L'éternel retour, La Danse de mort, Dédée d'Anvers, L'Aigle à deux têtes, Miquette et sa mère, The Beggars' Opera* (Brook, Britain, 53, also costumes), *Ali Baba, La Femme et le pantin, Marie-Octobre, Le Crime ne paie pas, Peau de banane, Le Journal d'une femme de chambre, Les Fêtes galantes, Echappement libre, Oscar, King Lear* (Brook, Britain/Denmark, 70).

397 WHEELER, René (1912 –). B: Paris. Scriptwriter and director. Has written the scenarios and dialogue for several films.

Main films: *La Cage aux rossignols, Jour de fête, La Vie en rose, Fanfan la Tulipe, L'Amour d'une femme, Du Rififi chez les hommes, Les Aventures de Till l'Espiègle*. Directed three unusual films of his own: *Premières armes, Châteaux en Espagne, Vers l'extase*.

398 WIENER, Jean (1896 –). B: Paris. Composer, who has scored several films since 1932; also song composer. His melodies have proved very popular. His daughter, Elisabeth Wiener, played in *La Prisonnière*.

Main film scores: *Les Affaires publiques, La Bandera, Le Crime de M. Lange* (co. Joseph Kosma), *Les Bas-fonds, Untel père et fils, Le Voyageur de la Toussaint, Panique, Macadam, Les Frères Bouquinquant, Le Point du jour, Rendez-vous de Juillet, French Cancan, Touchez pas au grisbi, La Femme et le pantin, Pantalaskas, Au hasard Balthazar, Révolution d'Octobre, Une Femme douce, Le petit théâtre de Jean Renoir* (co. KOSMA).

399 WILSON, Georges (1921 –). B: Champigny-sur-Marne. Actor and director (both theatre and cinema). Studied music. 1950 – 52: Comédie-Française. For the next decade he worked, often as stage producer, with Jean Vilar at the TNP.

Main films (as actor): *La Jument verte, Le Dialogue des Carmélites, Terrain vague, Le Farceur, Une aussi longue absence, Léviathan, Mélodie en sous-sol, Mandrin, La noia* (Damiani, Italy, 63), *Dragées au poivre, Lo straniero* (Visconti, Italy/France/Algeria, 67), *C'era una volta* (Rosi, Italy, 67), *Max et les ferrailleurs*.

400 ZECCA, Ferdinand (1864 – 1947). B. and D: Paris. An important director in the early days of Pathé. At first singer (from 1899). From 1905: producer only. His work was realistic in its depiction of social conditions.

Main films: *Histoire d'une crime, Tempête dans une chambre à coucher, Les Victimes de l'alcoolisme, La Grève, La Passion, L'Affaire Dreyfus, La Fièvre de l'or*.

Jean Renoir's LA MARSEILLAISE, with sets designed by Georges Wakhévitch

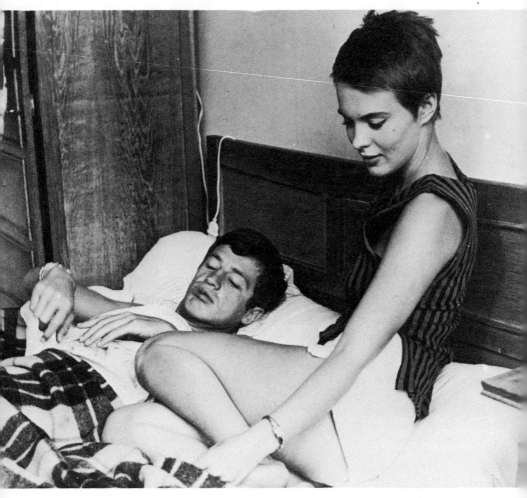

Jean-Paul Belmondo and Jean Seberg in A BOUT DE SOUFFLE

Index

Note: the index includes only French films, except for films shot abroad by French *cinéastes*, and films shot in France by foreign *cinéastes* based in the country (Ivens, Borowczyk, Klein etc.).

Feature films only are listed, save for a handful of very famous shorts. The dates of short films appear in the filmographies (as do those of any foreign film cited, together with the director's name).

The entry number in **bold** type after each title in the Index refers to the director's filmography.

An asterisk before a title indicates that the film is still in production at press-date and may change its name subsequently.

For reasons of space, the following articles have been omitted from the Index: *le, la, les, l', ce, cette, ces, un, une, de, du,* and *des.*

A

A Bout de souffle/Breathless (1960) 44, 51, 74, 134, **200**, 278, 391.

Abus de confiance (1937) **144**, 379, 380.

A Cause, à cause d'une femme (1962) 108, **154**, 388

Accident (1962) **202**.

A cœur joie/Two Weeks in September (1967) 38, **76**, 265, 354, 369.

Adelaïde/The Depraved (1968) **359**.

Adieu l'ami (1968) 148, 184, **210**.

Adieu Léonard (1943) 79, 316, **317**.

Adieu Philippine (1961) 44, **346**.

Adorable menteuse (1961) 154, **394**.

A double tour/Web of Passion (1959) 51, **105**, 143, 174, 194, 241, 335.

Affaire du courrier de Lyon (1937, Maurice Lehmann) 27, 165.

Affaire est dans le sac (1932) 85, 95, 221, 251, 316, **317**, 373.

Affaire Maurizius/On Trial (1953) **168**, 195, 335, 379, 380.

Affaires publiques (1934) **81**, 398.

A fleur de peau (1963) **58**.

Age d'or (1930) 31, 80, 85, **86**, 282.

Agence matrimoniale (1951) **251**.

Aigle à deux têtes (1947) 55, **125**, 180, 268, 273, 396.

Ailes brisées (1932) **61**.

Aimez-vous les femmes?/Do You Like Women? (1964, Jean Léon) 390.

Aîné des Ferchaux (1962) 51, 143, 146, **278**, 349, 379.

Air de Paris (1954) 16, **96**, 187, 213, 358, 371.

*Albatros (1971) **281**.

Alerte en Méditerranée (1938) **224**.

Alexandre le bienheureux (1969) 83, 225, 294, **334**.

Ali Baba et les 40 voleurs (1954) **46**, 176, 396.

Alibi (1937) 1, **110**, 226, 262, 366.

All about Loving *see* Amour.

Aller simple (1970) **197**.

Allez France! (1964) **156**.

Alliance (1970) 98, **106**, 228.

All the Gold in the World *see* Tout l'or du monde.

Alphaville (1965) 134, **200**, 228.

Amant de cinq jours/Infidelity (1960) 74, **84**, 100, 146, 315.

Amant de Lady Chatterley/Lady Chatterley's Lover (1955) **7**.

Amants (1958) 136, 143, 174, **266**, 282, 285.

Amants de Bras-Mort (1950) 130, 213, **302**.

Amazing Monsieur Fabre *see* Monsieur Fabre.

Amants de Teruel (1961) **343**.

Amants de Vérone (1948) 3, 5, 79, 97, **103**, 137, 236, 316, 322.

Amélie ou le temps d'aimer (1961) **161**, 274, 292.

Américain (1970, Marcel Bozzuffi) 184, 357, 374.

America through the Keyhole *see* Amérique insolite.

Amérique insolite/America through the Keyhole (1958) 80, 203, 254, **323**.

Ames de fous (1918) **164**.

*Amis (1971) **63**.

Amitiés particulières (1964) 27, 75, **145**.

Amour avec des si (1963) **255**.

Amour/All about Loving (1964) **26**, 312.

Yves Montand in L'AVEU

Josette Day and Jean Marais in LA BELLE ET LE BÊTE

B

Babette s'en va-t-en guerre (1959) 38, 65, 108, **114**, 177, 257, 370.

Bachelor Girl, The *see* Garçonne.

Baie des anges/Bay of Angels (1963) **150**, 254, 285.

Baiser (1929) **181**.

Baisers volés/Stolen Kisses (1968) 147, 250, 356, **376**.

Baker's Wife, The *see* Femme du boulanger.

Bal des pompiers (1948) **61**.

Bal du comte d'Orgel (1970) **7**, 82, 273.

Ballade pour un chien (1968) 379, **385**.

Ballade pour un voyou (1962) 35, **71**, 290, 294, 369.

Balle au cœur (1965) **314**.

Balle dans le canon (1958) **154**, 362.

Ballet mécanique (1924) **253**.

Ballon rouge (1956) **244**, 354.

Balthazar *see* Au Hasard Balthazar.

Bande à part/The Outsiders (1964) 78, 134, 185, **200**, 228, 254.

Bandera (1935) 11, **168**, 187, 237, 282, 327, 337, 364, 398.

Barrabas (1920) **179**.

Barbarella (1969) 141, 220, 265, 325, **377**.

Barbouzes (1964) 65, 139, **249**.

Baron de l'Ecluse (1959) 22, **145**, 187, 301, 315.

Baron fantôme (1943, Serge de Poligny) 125, 136.

Barrage contre le Pacifique/The Sea Wall/This Angry Age (1958) **119**, 167.

Bas-fonds/The Lower Depths (1936) 20, 129, 187, 226, 262, **326**, 364, 398.

Bataille de France (1964) **26**.

Bataille de San Sebastian/Guns for San Sebastian (1969) **386**.

Bataille du rail (1946) 5, 41, **119**.

Bateau (1970, Gérard Brach) 100.

Battements de cœur (1939) 20, 140, 141, **144**, 372.

Bay of Angels *see* Baie des anges.

Beau monstre (1970, Sergio Gobbi) 32, 83.

Beau Serge/Handsome Serge (1958) 63, 82, **105**, 143, 241, 295, 391.

Beauté du diable (1949) 40, **118**, 232, 274, 282, 311, 360.

Beauty and the Beast *see* Belle et la bête.

Bébert et l'omnibus/The Holy Terror (1963) 33, **334**.

Bel âge/Love Is When You Make It (1958) 49, 82, 83, 122, 146, 158, **230**, 302, 318, 390.

Bel ami (1954) **138**, 387.

Belle américaine (1961) 123, **156**, 157, 186.

Belle de jour (1966) 65, **86**, 98, 120, 151, 269, 312, 390.

Belle ensorceleuse (1941) **118**, 272.

Belle équipe (1936) **168**, 187, 237, 321, 337, 363, 379.

Belle et la bête/Beauty and the Beast (1945) 5, 21, 28, 55, **119**, **125**, 268, 308.

Belle meunière (1948) **303**.

Belle Nivernaise (1924) **171**.

Belle vie/The Good Life (1962) **170**, 391.

Belles de nuit/Night Beauties (1952) 40, 97, **118**, 311, 370, 380.

Benito Gereno (1969) 255, **344**.

Benjamin (1967) 120, 123, 147, 151, **154**, 287, 312, 388.

Bergère et le ramoneur (1952) **204**, 236, 316.

Bertrand Cœur de Lion (1950) **156**.

Bête humaine (1938) 95, 187, 236, 262, **326**, 361.

Between Love and Duty *see* Bois des amants.

Biches/The Does (1968) 23, **105**, 194, 374.

Big Day, The *see* Jour de fête.

Big Risk, The *see* Classe tous risques.

Bijoutiers du clair de lune/Heaven Fell That Night (1957) 28, 38, 257, 370, **377**.

Birds Come To Die in Peru, The *see* Oiseaux vont mourir au Pérou.

Biribi (1971, Daniel Moosmann) 66.

Black Orpheus *see* Orfeu negro.

Black Torpedoes, The *see* Peau de torpedo.

Black Tulip, The *see* Tulipe noire.

*Blanche (1971) **72**, 120, 360.

Blazing Sun *see* Plein soleil.

Blé en herbe/Ripening Seed (1953) 27, **30**, 160, 180, 186.

Bloko (1966) **239**.

Blood and Roses *see* Et mourir de plaisir.

Bluebeard *see* Landru.

Bob le flambeur (1955) 143, **278**.

*BOF Anatomie d'un livreur (1971, Claude Faraldo) 162.

Bois des amants/Between Love and Duty (1960) 27, **30**, 160, 339, 369.

Bon Dieu sans confession (1953) **30**, 33, 140, 160.

Bonheur/Happiness (1964) 45, 147, **381**.

Bonjour sourire (1955) **350**.

Bonne occase (1964) 65, **161**.

Bonne soupe (1964, Robert Thomas) 48, **195**, 198.

Jean-Claude Drouot with his two children in LE BONHEUR

Bonnes causes (1963) 79, **114**, 394.
Bonnes femmes (1959) 23, **105**, 143, 194, 241.
Borsalino (1970) 51, 75, 98, 148, **153**, 350.
Boucher (1970) 23, **105**.
Boudu sauvé des eaux/Boudu Saved from Drowning (1932) 87, **326**, 360.
Boudu Saved from Drowning *see* Boudu sauvé des eaux.
Boule de suif (1945) 40, **114**, 222, 273, 315, 360.
*Boulevard du rhum (1971) 38, 160, **170**, 384.
Bourse et la vie/Money or Your Life (1965) **281**.

Brain, The *see* Cerveau.
Branquignols (1949) **156**.
Break the News *see* Fausses nouvelles.
Breathless *see* A bout de souffle.
Bride sur le cou/Please, Not Now! (1961) 26, 38, 78, 139, 184, 372, **377**.
Bride Wore Black, The *see* Mariée était en noir.
Brigitte et Brigitte (1965) **288**.
British Sounds (1968) **200**.
Brumes d'automne (1926) **233**.
Bye bye Barbara (1969) **154**.

C

Cage aux filles (1949) **121**.
Cage aux rossignols (1943, Jean Dréville) 122, 397.
Cage de verre (1965) **19**.
Calcutta (1968) **266**.
Camarades (1970) **229**.
*Camisards (1971) **9**.
*Ça n'arrive qu'aux autres (1971) 151, **375**.
Candide (1960) **94**, 100, 186, 360, 372.
Cannabis (1969, Pierre Koralnik) 188, 238.
Capitaine Fracasse (1927, Cavalcanti) **101**
Capitaine Fracasse (1942, Gance) **189**.
Caporal épinglé/The Vanishing Corporal (1961) 78, 100, 236, **326**, 330.
Caprices de Marie (1970) 74, **84**.
Carabiniers/The Soldiers (1962) 19, 44, 134, **200**.
*Caravane d'amour (1971) **323**.
Carmelites, The *see* Dialogue des Carmélites.
Carmen (1926, Feyder) **181**, 276.
Carmen (1943, Christian-Jaque) **114**, 337.
Carnaval (1953) **303**.
Carnet du bal (1937) 2, 42, 48, 64, **168**, 176, 221, 222, 226, 232, 319, 339, 367.
Carnival des vérités (1920) **258**.
Carnival in Flanders *see* Kermesse héroïque.
Caroline chérie (1950, Richard Pottier) 13, 97.
Carrefour des enfants perdus (1943) 14, 29, **224**.
Carrosse d'or (1952) 325, **326**.

Cartouche (1961) 51, 74, **84**, 137, 146, 273, 364, 388.
Cas du Dr. Laurent/The Case of Dr. Laurent (1956) 187, **251**.
Case of Dr. Laurent, The *see* Cas du Dr. Laurent.
Casque d'or (1951) **46**, 49, 88, 129, 141, 169, 274, 282, 308, 322, 357, 380.
Casino de Paris (1957) **214**.
*Casse (1971) 51, 325, 349, **386**.
Cassius le grand (1967) **234**.
Cela s'appelle l'aurore (1955) **86**, 160, 177, 236, 248, 269, 282.
Celui qui doit mourir/He Who Must Die (1956, Jules Dassin) 28, 56, 338, 355.
Centinela alerta (1935) **201**.
Cent mille dollars au soleil (1964) 66, 384, **386**.
Cercle rouge (1970) 77, 143, 148, 278, **280**, 284.
Certains l'aiment froide (1960, Jean Bastia) 65.
Cerveau/The Brain (1968) 51, 77, 146, **300**, 370.
César (1933) 183, **303**, 319.
César Grandblaise (1970) **155**.
Ce soir ou jamais (1961) **154**, 159, 228, 330.
C'est arrivé demain/It Happened Tomorrow (1944) **118**, 353.
Chagrin et la pitié (1971) **297**.
Chamade/Heartbeat (1968) **102**, 151, 312, 350.
Champagne Murders, The *see* Scandale.
Chance et l'amour (1965) **59**, 65.

Corinne Marchand in CLÉO DE 5 À 7

Paul Meurisse and Catherine Rouvel in LE DÉJEUNER SUR L'HERBE

Michel Simon and Louis Jouvet in DRÔLE DE DRAME

E

Jean-Pierre Cargol and François Truffaut in L'ENFANT SAUVAGE

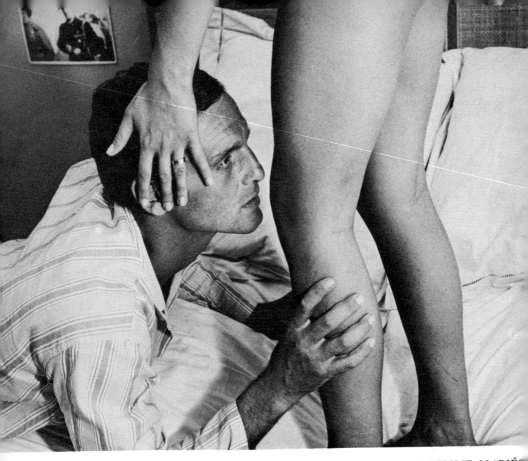

Philippe Leroy and the legs of Macha Méril in Godard's UNE FEMME MARIÉ

Françoise Prévost and Mireille Darc in GALIA

Jacques Doniol-Valcroze with François Brion in L'IMMORTELLE

Hoa-Binh (1969) **134**, 391.
Hole, The *see* Trou.
Holy Terror, The *see* Bébert et l'omnibus.
Homme à l'Hispano (1933, Jean Epstein) 48, 396.
*Homme au cerveau greffé (1971) **158**, 374.
Homme au chapeau rond/The Eternal Husband (1946, Pierre Billon) 319.
Homme aux cléfs d'or (1956) 183, 198, **224**.
Homme de désir (1970) **149**, 331.
Homme de Marrakech (1966) **153**.
Homme de nulle part (1937) **110**.
Homme de Rio/That Man from Rio (1963) 51, 74, **84**, 146, 159, 354, 355.
Homme de trop (1966) 63, 78, 120, **193**, 312, 379.
Homme du large (1920) **258**.
Homme du Sud (1944) 262, **326**.

Homme et une femme/A Man and a Woman (1966) 3, 80, 242, **255**.
Homme marche dans la ville (1949) 209, 293, **302**.
Homme-orchestre (1970) **235**.
Homme qui ment (1968) **333**, 374.
Homme qui me plaît (1969) 51, 198, 242, **255**.
Honneurs de la guerre (1960) 123, **155**.
Honour among Thieves *see* Touchez pas au grisbi.
Horizon (1966) 134, 188, **342**.
Hôtel du Nord (1938) 11, 16, 25, 66, **96**, 163, 221, 222, 226, 370.
House of Lovers *see* Pot-bouille.
Huit-clos/Vicious Circle (1954) 16, **24**, 248.
Huitième jour (1959) **208**, 236, 331.
*Humeur vagabonde (1971) 35, 75, **264**.

I

Idiot (1946, Georges Lampin) 40, 273, 286, 311, 364, 367, 371.
Idiot à Paris/Idiot in Paris (1967) 66, **235**, 241, 242.
Idiot in Paris *see* Idiot à Paris.
Idoles (1968, Marc'O) 296.
I Have a New Master *see* Ecole buissonnière.
I Killed Rasputin *see* J'ai tué Raspoutine.
Iles enchantées (1965) 120, **393**.
Ils (1970) **359**, 379.
Ils étaient neuf célibataires (1939) **206**, 286.
Image (1925) **181**.
I Married a Witch *see* Ma femme est une sorcière.
Immortal Story, The *see* Histoire immortelle.
Immortelle (1962) 83, 146, 147, 158, **333**.
Inconnus dans la maison/Strangers in the House (1942) 124, **144**, 273, 372.

Inconnus de la terre (1962) **347**.
Indiscret (1969) 255, **323**.
Inévitable M. Dubois (1943, Pierre Billon) 129.
Infidelity *see* Amant de cinq jours.
Ingénue libertine (1950) **24**, 203.
Inhumaine (1923) 30, 101, **258**.
Inondation (1924) **147**.
Insoumis (1964) **102**, 146, 148, 174, 325.
Isle of Sinners *see* Dieu a besoin des hommes.
Is Paris Burning? *see* Paris brûle-t-il?
It Happened Tomorrow *see* C'est arrivé demain.
It's Hot in Hell *see* Singe en hiver.
It's My Life *see* Vivre sa vie.

J

J'accuse (1918 and 1938) 87, **189**.
Jaguar (1956/68) **341**.
J'ai dix-sept ans (1945) **61**.
J'ai tué Raspoutine/I Killed Rasputin (1967) **212**, 367.

Jean de la lune (1932, Jean Choux) 1, 25, 310, 324, 360.
Jeff (1969) 139, 148, **210**.
Jenny (1936) 39, **96**, 169, 213, 236, 316, 339, 379.
Jérôme Perreau (1936) **189**.

Francine Bergé in JUDEX (1963)

K

L

Marc Michel and Anouk Aimée in LOLA

Antoine Vitez and Françoise Fabian in MA NUIT CHEZ MAUD

Gérard Philipe and Lili Palmer in MONTPARNASSE 1

N

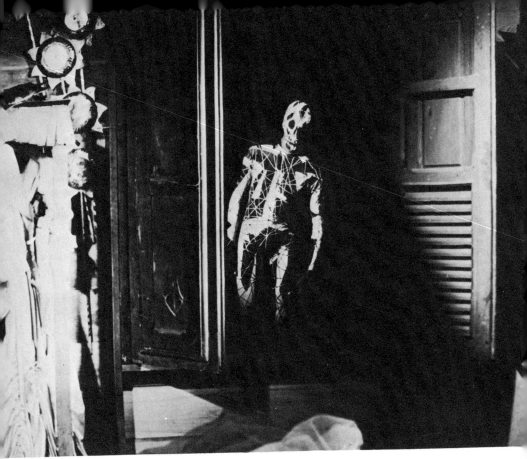

A stunning shot from ORFEU NEGRO

Nana (1955) **114**.

Naples au baiser de feu (1937, Augusto Genina) 36, 337, 360.

Napoléon (1927) 11, 17, 18, 62, 87, 140, **189**, 211, 213, 237.

Napoléon (1954) 186, 187, **206**, 268, 284, 287, 315, 366.

Nathalie agent secret (1959) 97, **144**.

Neige sur les pas (1941) **61**.

Nick Carter (1913/14) **207**.

Night Beauties *see* Belles de nuit.

Night Is My Kingdom *see* Nuit est mon royaume.

Night Is Not for Sleep *see* Toi le venin.

Noces de sable/Daughter of the Sands (1948, André Zwobada) 33.

Nommé la Rocca (1961) **47**, 51, 123.

No Questions on Sunday *see* Pas question le Samedi.

Notre-Dame de Paris (1911) **93**.

Notre-Dame de Paris (1956) **68**, 145, 316.

Nous les gosses (1941) 34, 88, **138**, 372.

Nous sommes tous des assassins/Are We All Murderers? (1952) **103**, 364.

Nouveau journal d'une femme en blanc (1965) **30**.

Nouveaux aristocrates (1961, Francis Rigaud) 139, 280.

Nouveaux Messieurs (1929) **181**, 310, 364.

Nouveaux riches (1938) **61**.

Nouvelle mission de Judex (1917) **179**.

Novices (1970, Guy Casaril) 38, 194, 198.

Nuit bulgare (1970, Michel Mitrani) 379, 390, 394.

Nuit de carrefour (1933) **326**, 327.

Nuit est mon royaume/Night Is My Kingdom (1951) 41, **240**, 300, 364.

Nuit et brouillard (1955) 123, 128, **328**.

Nuit fantastique (1942) 109, 222, **258**, 315, 371.

Nuits des espions (1959) **212**, 394.

O

Objectif 500 millions (1966) 44, **351**.

Occupe-toi d'Amélie/Oh, Amelia (1949) 27, **30**, 33, 95, 140, 160.

October Revolution *see* Révolution d'Octobre.

Octobre à Madrid (1965) **208**.

Octobre à Paris (1962) **305**.

Œil du malin (1961) 23, **105**, 108.

Œil du Monocle (1962) **249**, 280.

Œil pour œil/An Eye for an Eye (1957) **103**.

Of Flesh and Blood *see* Grands chemins.

Oh, Amelia *see* Occupe-toi d'Amélie.

Oiseau de Paradis (1962) **90**.

Oiseux vont mourir au Pérou/The Birds Come To Die in Peru (1968, Romain Gary) 79, 140, 273, 338.

Oldest Profession in the World, The *see* Plus vieux métier du monde.

Old Guard *see* Vieux de la vieille.

Olivia (1950) **24**, 361.

On a volé la Joconde (1965) **154**, 394.

On a volé un homme (1934) **298**.

One American Movie (1969) **200**.

One Plus One (1968) **200**.

*On est toujours trop bon avec les femmes (1971) **69**.

On n'enterre pas le Dimanche (1960) 147, **161**.

On purge Bébé (1931) 80, **326**, 360.

On Trial *see* Affaire Maurizius.

Ophélia (1962) **105**.

Orage (1937) 1, **7**, 287.

Orchid for the Tiger, A *see* Tigre se parfume à la dynamite.

Order of the Daisy *see* Compagnons de la marguerite.

Or des mers (1932) **171**, 273.

Or du duc (1965) **37**, 198, 330, 372.

Orfeu negro/Black Orpheus (1958) **90**.

Orgueilleux/The Proud Ones (1953) **8**, 257, 287, 311.

Orphée (1949) 28, 68, 100, **125**, 169, 209, 268, 278, 281, 308.

Orpheline (1921) **179**.

O salto (1967) **106**, 391.

Georges Rivière (at right) in LE PASSAGE DU RHIN

Os bandeirantes (1960) **90**.
Oscar (1968) 186, **283**, 396.
Other One, The *see* Une et l'autre.
Ours (1960) **354**.

Ours et la poupée (1969) 38, 100, **154**.
*Out One (1971) 296, **332**.
Outsiders, The *see* Bande à part.

P

Panic *see* Panique.
Panique/Panic (1946) **168**, 209, 337, 360, 364, 398.
Pantalaskas (1959) 95, **309**, 398.
*Panthères blanches (1971) **223**.
Papa, Mama, the Maid and I *see* Papa, Maman, la bonne et moi.
Papa, Maman, la bonne et moi/Papa, Mama, the Maid and I (1954) 186, **251**, 372.
Papa, Maman, ma femme et moi (1955) **251**, 372.
Paradis perdu (1939) **189**.
Parapluies de Cherbourg/The Umbrellas of Cherbourg (1963) 147, **150**, 151, 174, 254, 387.
Pardonnez nos offenses/Forgive Us Our Trespasses (1956) 126, **212**, 257, 394.
Parents terribles/The Storm Within (1948) 28, 55, **125**, 232, 268.
Parfum de la dame en noir (1949) 49, **138**.
Parias de la gloire (1963) **144**.
Paris Belongs to Us *see* Paris nous appartient.
Paris brûle-t-il?/Is Paris Burning? (1966) 27, 51, 100, **119**, 141, 148, 203, 220, 284, 357, 374.
Paris Deauville (1935) **145**.
Paris in the Raw *see* Femme spectacle.
Paris 1900 (1947) **383**.
Paris n'existe pas (1969) **52**, 188.
Paris nous appartient/Paris Belongs to Us (1958) 19, 82, 318, **332**, 376.
Paris qui dort/The Crazy Ray (1924) **118**.
Paris vu par . . ./Six in Paris (1965) 23, **105**, **200**, **336**, **341**, 352.
Parisette (1921) **179**.
Parisienne (1957) 26, 38, **69**, 395.
Parisiennes (1961) **7**, 65, **69**.
Partie de campagne (1936) 80, 85, 236, 316, 321, 325, **326**.

Par un beau matin d'été (1964) **153**.
Pas de caviar pour Tante Olga (1965) **47**, 65.
Pas question le Samedi/No Questions on Sunday (1964, Alex Joffé) 177.
Passage du Rhin/The Crossing of the Rhine (1960) 32, **103**, 130.
Passager de la pluie (1969) **119**, 225.
Passe du Diable (1956) **351**.
Passion de Jeanne d'Arc (1928, Carl Dreyer) 175, 272, 361.
Patates (1970) **30**, 160.
Patrie (1945) 12, 64, 73, **138**.
Patrouille Anderson (1967) **351**.
Patrouille de choc (1957) **58**.
Pattes blanches (1948) 2, 13, 57, **201**, 367.
Pattes de mouches (1936) **201**.
Paul (1969) **275**.
Paulina s'en va (1969, André Téchiné) 296.
Pavé de Paris/The Pavements of Paris (1961) **144**.
Pavements of Paris, The *see* Pavé de Paris.
Pays de Cocagne (1970) **172**.
Pays d'où je viens (1956) 1, 17, 78, **96**.
Pays sans étoiles (1945) 79, **240**, 301, 389.
Peau d'âne (1971) 123, **150**, 151, 254, 268, 315, 356.
Peau de banane (1963) 51, 74, **297**, 350, 396.
Peau d'espion (1966) 66, **283**.
Peau de torpedo/Black Torpedoes (1970) 23, **145**, 354.
Peau douce/Silken Skin (1964) 134, 146, 159, **376**.
Peau et les os/The Mazur File (1960) 63, **305**, 391.
Pêcheur d'Islande (1959) **351**.
Pension Mimosas (1935) 16, 57, **181**, 213, 276, 321, 339, 364.
Pépé le Moko (1936) 36, 137, **168**, 187, 222, 237, 282, 321, 337.

Jacques Tati in PLAYTIME

Nora Gregor and Jean Renoir in LA RÈGLE DU JEU

Q

Quai des brumes/Port of Shadows (1938) 79, **96**, 187, 221, 287, 316, 321, 353, 360, 373.

Quai des Orfèvres (1947) 88, **124**, 160, 165, 177, 226, 370.

Quand passent les faisans (1965) 280, **283**.

Quand tu liras cette lettre (1952) **278**.

48 h. d'amour (1969, Cécil Saint-Laurent) 296.

Quatorze-dix-huit (1962) **26**.

Quatorze Juillet (1933) 11, **110**, 221, 276, 282, 310.

Quatre cents coups/The 400 Blows (1959) 82, 143, 174, 250, 290, **376**.

*Quatre nuits d'un rêveur (1971) **81**.

Quatre vérités/Three Fables of Love (1962) **118**, 228.

Que la bête meure/Killer! (1969) **105**, 194.

Quelle joie de vivre (1961) **119**, 143, 148.

Question of Rape, A see Viol.

Qui? (1970, Léonard Keigel) 338.

Qui êtes-vous M. Sorge?/Who Are You? (1961) **115**.

Qui êtes-vous Polly Maggoo?/Who Are You Polly Maggoo? (1965) 185, **234**, 254, 294, 391.

R

Rage au corps (1953, Ralph Habib) 17.

Ramuntcho (1958) **351**.

Rapace (1968) **197**, 384.

Raphaël ou le débauché (1971) **154**, 338, 392.

Raspoutine (1953, Georges Combret) 40.

Rat d'Amérique (1962) **4**, 32.

Ravishing idiot, A see Ravissante idiote.

Ravissante idiote/A Ravishing Idiot (1963) 38, **283**.

Razzia sur la schnouf (1954) 137, **144**, 187, 384.

Récompense (1965) **76**.

Recours en grâce (1959, Lazlo Benedek) 198, 220, 331.

Red Inn, The see Auberge rouge.

Reflux (1961) **194**.

Regain/Harvest (1937) 176, 286, **303**.

Regards sur la folie (1962) **347**.

Régates de San Francisco (1959) 27, **30**, 160, 369, 370.

Règle du jeu/Rules of the Game (1939) 34, 95, 137, 163, 236, 262, 282, **326**.

Religieuse (1965) 44, 228, 315, **332**.

Remontons les Champs-Elysées (1938) **206**.

Remorques (1941) 103, 187, **201**, 287, 316, 321, 324, 370, 373.

Renaissance (1966) **347**.

Rencontres (1962) **2**.

Rendezvous at Midnight see Rendez-vous de minuit.

Revenant (1946) 109, **114**, 211, 226, 286.

Rendez-vous de minuit/Rendezvous at Midnight (1961) 21, 35, **252**, 338.

Rendez-vous de Juillet (1949) **46**, 130, 195, 325, 338, 398.

Renegade Priest, The see Défroqué.

Repos du guerrier (1962) 38, 212, 265, 370, **377**.

Republic of Sin see Fièvre monte à El Pao.

Requiem pour un caïd (1964) **121**.

Retour à la vie (1948) **103**, **124**.

Révélateur (1968) **190**.

Révolution d'Octobre/October Revolution (1967) **340**, 398.

Rideau cramoisi/The Crimson Circle (1951) 3, **20**, 274, 295, 353.

Rien que les heures (1923) **101**.

Rififi à Tokyo (1961) **153**, 197, 379.

Rififi chez les hommes (1954, Jules Dassin) 2, 28, 212, 355, 397.

Ripening Seed see Blé en herbe.

Risques du métier (1967) **103**, 331.

River see Fleuve.

Road to Corinth, The see Route de Corinthe.

Road to Katmandu, The see Chemins de Katmandou.

Roger la Honte (1946) **103**.

Rogopag (1962) **200**.

Roi de cœur/King of Hearts (1966) 74, 79, **84**, 146, 315.

Roi du cirque (1925) **259**.

Annie Girardot in LA PROIE POUR L'OMBRE

Simone Signoret (at right) in LES SORCIÈRES DE SALEM

Emmanuelle Riva and Jean Servais in THOMAS L'IMPOSTEUR

Témoin dans la ville (1959) **283**.

Tempête dans une chambre à coucher (1901) **400**.

Temps de mourir (1970, André Farwagi) 238.

Temps des assassins (1963) **168**.

Temps des loups/Dillinger 70 (1969, Sergio Gobbi) 32.

Temps des œufs durs (1957) **94**.

Temps de vivre (1969) **307**, 394.

Temps du ghetto (1961) **340**.

Temps fou (1970) **90**.

Tendre ennemie (1936) 14, **298**, 353.

Tendre voyou (1967) **47**, 51, 354.

Teresa (1970) **385**.

Terrain vague (1960) **96**, 254, 325, 399.

Terre (1921) **14**.

Terre sans pain/Las Hurdes (1932) **86**, 261.

Testament d'Orphée (1959) 17, 38, 199, **125**, 195, 268, 376.

Testament du Dr Cordelier/Experiment in Evil (1959) 39, 184, 236, 282, **326**.

Tête contre les murs/The Keepers (1958) 3, 32, 79, **182**, 220, 280, 281, 353.

Tête d'un homme (1932) **168**, 396.

That Man from Rio see Homme de Rio.

Théâtre de M. et Mme Kabal/The Concert of Monsieur and Madame Kabal (1967) **72**.

Thérèse Etienne (1957) **246**.

Thérèse Desqueyroux (1962) **182**, 185, 220, 273, 294, 331.

Thérèse Raquin (1928) **181**.

Thérèse Raquin (1953) **96**, 357, 364, 367, 371.

These Things Happen see Choses de la vie.

This Angry Age see Barrage contre le Pacifique.

Thomas l'imposteur/Thomas the Imposter (1964) 28, 32, **182**, 331, 355.

Thomas the Imposter see Thomas l'imposteur.

Thou Shalt Not Kill see Tu ne tueras point.

Three Fables of Love, The see Quatre vérités.

Three Women see Trois femmes.

Tiger Likes Fresh Meat see Tigre aime la chair fraîche.

Tigre aime la chair fraîche/Tiger Likes Fresh Meat (1964) **105**.

Tigre se parfume à la dynamite/A Orchid for the Tiger (1965) **105**.

Tih-Minh (1918) **179**.

Time To Live and a Time To Die, A see Feu follet.

Tire au flanc (1928) 34, 80, **326**, 360.

Tire au flanc (1961) **199**, 241, 376.

Tirez sur le pianiste (1960) 56, 74, 80, 134, 146, 162, 290, **376**.

Toi le venin (1958) **212**, 388, 394.

Toni (1934) 325, **326**.

Tonnerre de Dieu/God's Thunder (1965) 203, **246**.

Tontons flingueurs/Crooks in Clover (1963) 22, 65, 66, 146, **249**, 330, 384.

Topaze (1934, Louis Gasnier) 226.

Topaze (1951) 176, **303**.

Topkapi (1964, Jules Dassin) 5.

Touchez pas au grisbi/Honour among Thieves (1953) **46**, 169, 187, 284, 285, 362, 398.

Tour de Nesle/The Tower of Lust (1954) **189**.

Tournant dangereux (1955, Robert Bibal) 337.

Tournoi (1929) **326**.

Tout l'or du monde/All the Gold in the World (1961) 40, 77, **118**, 159, 294, 330, 380.

Toutes folles de lui (1966) **94**.

Tower of Lust, The see Tour de Nesle.

*Trafic (1971) **368**.

Tragédie impériale (1938) **258**.

Train des suicidés (1931) **202**.

Train sans yeux (1926) **101**.

Traité de bave et d'éternité (1951) **218**.

Traité du rossignol (1970, Jean Fléchet) 83.

Trans-Europ-Express (1966) 238, **333**, 374.

Trap for Cinderella, A see Piège pour Cendrillon.

Travailleurs de la mer (1918) **14**.

Traversée de Paris/Four Bags Full (1956) 27, **30**, 77, 160, 186, 187.

Treize jours en France (1968) 242, **255**, **323**.

Trêve/The Truce (1969, Claude Guillemot) 152, 195.

Trial of Joan of Arc, The see Procès de Jeanne d'Arc.

Tribulations d'un Chinois en Chine/Up to His Ears (1965) 51, 74, **84**, 354, 379.

Tricheurs/Youthful Sinners (1958) 51, **96**, 325, 358, 369.

Tripes au soleil (1959) **58**, 68.

Trois chambres à Manhattan (1965) **96**, 198, 338, 353, 358.

Trois femmes/Three Women (1951, André Michel) 380.

Trois hommes sur un cheval (1969) **290**.

Trois mousquetaires (1953) 77, 157, **214**.

317ème Section (1964) 44, 134, **351**.

Samy Frey and Brigitte Bardot in LA VÉRITÉ

Trop petit mon ami (1970, Eddy Matalon) 78.
Trou/The Hole (1960) 26, **46**, 123, 197.
Truce, The *see* Trêve.
Truth, The *see* Vérité.
Truth about Our Marriage, The *see* Vérité sur Bébé
Donge.
Tu es Pierre (1959) **2**.
Tu imagines Robinson (1969) **314**, 352.
Tulipe noir/The Black Tulip (1963) 65, **114**, 143,
148.

Tu ne tueras point/Thou Shalt Not Kill (1960) 27,
30, 160.
25th Hour, The *see* Vingt-cinquième heure.
Twenty-Four Hours in a Woman's Life *see* Vingt-
quatre heures de la vie d'une femme.
Two Are Guilty *see* Glaive et la balance.
Two of Us, The *see* Vieil homme et l'enfant.
Two Weeks in September *see* A Cœur joie.
Typhon sur Nagasaki (1956) **115**, 268, 395.

U

Umbrellas of Cherbourg, The *see* Parapluies de
Cherbourg.
Une et l'autre/The Other One (1967) **9**, 141, 188,
294, 318.
*Un Peu de soleil dans l'eau froide (1971) 153.

Un Peu, beaucoup, passionnément (1971) 170, 338.
Untel père et fils (1940) 1, **168**, 226, 237, 287, 319,
364, 398.
Up to His Ears *see* Tribulations d'un Chinois en
Chine.

V

Vacances de M. Hulot/Monsieur Hulot's Holiday
(1952) 299, **368**.
Vacances portugaises (1962) 17, 21, 25, 83, 134, 146,
151, 158, 195, **230**, 318.
Vache et le prisonnier (1959) 176, 222, **386**.
Valparaiso, Valparaiso (1970, Pascal Aubier) 136,
241.
Vampire de Dusseldorf (1964) 44, **212**.
Vampires (1916) **179**, 291.
Vampyr (1932, Carl Dreyer) 272.
Vanishing Corporal, The *see* Caporal épinglé.
Variétés (1935, Nikolas Farkas) 11, 187.
Vent d'Est (1969) **200**.
Vénus aveugle (1940) **189**, 337.
Verdun vision d'histoire (1930) 62.
Vérité/The Truth (1960) 38, **124**, 185, 257, 280, 292,
370, 379.
Vérité sur Bébé Donge/The Truth about Our
Marriage (1951) 87, 140, **144**, 187.

Versailles *see* Si Versailles m'était conté.
Vers l'extase (1960) **397**.
Very Private Affair, A *see* Vie privée.
Veuve en or (1969) **22**, 169, 330.
Vice and Virtue *see* Vice et la vertu.
Vice et la vertu/Vice and Virtue (1962) 151, 198, 203,
212, 265, **377**.
Vicious Circle *see* Huis-clos.
Victims of Vice *see* Amour à la chaîne.
Victoire sur l'Anapurna (1955) **215**.
Vie (1957) **20**, 274, 325.
Vie à l'envers/Life Upside-Down (1964) 152, **223**.
Vie commence demain (1949) **383**.
Vie conjugale (1962) **103**, 108, 292.
Vie de château (1965) 79, 102, 147, 151, 254, 294,
320, 349, 350.
Vie d'un honnête homme (1952) 34, **206**, 360.
Vie en rose (1947, Jean Faurez) 380, 397.
Vie est à nous (1936) **326**.

Brigitte Bardot and Marcello Mastroianni in VIE PRIVÉE

Violence in the streets: a shot from Costa Gavras's Z